Books are t
th

D0296894

CAPITALISM AND IMPERIALISM

An Introduction to Neo-Marxian Concepts

IRVING M. ZEITLIN

University of Toronto

MARKHAM PUBLISHING COMPANY / **Chicago**

MARKHAM SOCIOLOGY SERIES
Robert W. Hodge, Editor

Adams, *Kinship in an Urban Setting*
Adams, *The American Family: A Sociological Interpretation*
Adams and Weirath, eds., *Readings on the Sociology of the Family*
Appelbaum, *Theories of Social Change*
Ash, *Social Movements in America*
Cole, *The Sociological Method*
Edwards, ed., *Sex and Society*
Farley, *Growth of the Black Population: A Study of Demographic Trends*
Filstead, ed., *An Introduction to Deviance: Readings on the Process of Making Deviants*
Filstead, ed., *Qualitative Methodology: Firsthand Involvement with the Social World*
Karp and Kelly, *Toward an Ecological Analysis of Intermetropolitan Migration*
Laumann, Siegel, and Hodge, eds., *The Logic of Social Hierarchies*
Lejeune, ed., *Class and Conflict in American Society*
Zeitlin, I., *Capitalism and Imperialism: An Introduction to Neo-Marxian Concepts*
Zeitlin, M., ed., *American Society, Inc.: Studies of the Social Structure and Political Economy of the United States*

Copyright © 1972 by Markham Publishing Company
All Rights Reserved
Printed in U.S.A.
Library of Congress Catalog Card No. 72–95718
Hardcover Standard Book Number 8410–4051–6
Paperback Standard Book Number 8410–4052–5

To Esther

Preface

In recent years the terms "capitalism," "corporate capitalism," and "imperialism" have again become conspicuous in political discourse. Mainly, of course, these terms have gained currency among radical critics of contemporary society. Nevertheless, little effort to explore these concepts in a systematic and scholarly fashion has been made within the universities.

This short essay is designed (a) to introduce the reader to these concepts and to the accompanying theoretical framework and (b) to demonstrate that they are not merely radical catchwords, but rather intellectually fruitful ideas that must be taken seriously in order to make sense of present-day social realities.

It should be stressed here that the present essay is for the most part intended as an expository work and does not pretend to break new ground. Whatever originality the essay might have lies in the knitting together of classical and contemporary ideas and highlighting the continuity between them. The result should illustrate clearly what might be meant by a so-called neo-Marxian analysis. The reader will notice that such an analysis involves one with history, political economy, political science, and sociology; hence, the analysis breaks out of the narrow and rigid confines of the separate academic disciplines as they are presently organized in the universities.

Perhaps this is the place to alert the reader to the fact that the beginning of the essay is in some ways the most difficult. The opening discussion introduces some of Marx's political-economic theories that may not be easy to grasp. However, I would ask the reader not to skip this part but to persist until he has understood it since it is essential to the entire argument that follows.

Finally, I disclaim any bibliographic comprehensiveness for the essay. To facilitate a smooth exposition, I have based my presentation on a few major books and have not cited the numerous articles and short essays dealing with the neo-Marxian concept of capitalism and imperialism.

I. Z.
March, 1972

Contents

1

Competitive Capitalism

For Karl Marx, the capitalist mode was revolutionary compared with all previous modes of production. Capitalists, as a class, could not but revolutionize the means of production and, with them, all other conditions of social existence. Capitalist accumulation brought with it the concentration and centralization of capital. Eventually, the accumulation of capital assumed the form of a conflict among capitals, with some winning and others losing, the latter being either destroyed or absorbed by the victors. The growth of capital in one enterprise was facilitated by the failure of others. As the costs of investment in *constant* capital increased (means of production and raw material) and the individual capitals already in the field expanded, fewer and fewer capitals were engaged in production. Hence, capital became increasingly concentrated.

The accumulation and concentration of capital and the

concomitant rise in the *organic composition of capital* [1] is also a battle of capitals using price competition as a major weapon. Each capitalist tries to cheapen his commodities. Other factors being equal, his success depends on the productivity of labor which, in turn, depends on the mass of means of production per worker: in short, on the scale of production.

Larger capitalists defeat the smaller ones, who then seek to enter the less modern spheres of industry where smaller investments in means of production are required. These defeated and smaller capitalists are numerous and weak. They enter industrial spheres that are lower in organic composition of capital and pay out more in variable capital than do their larger counterparts. Because operating expenses of the smaller capitalists are high, their enterprises are not competitive and they fail frequently. Some of their assets are absorbed by their larger competitors, and some simply vanish. These developments are accompanied by the *tendency* of the *rate* of profit to fall.

THE TENDENCY OF THE RATE OF PROFIT TO FALL

For Marx, then, capitalist development proceeds from small to large capitals, from diffuse to concentrated capitals, and

[1] Marx distinguished *constant* from *variable* capital: the first term refers to the money outlay for machines and raw material and the second to wages only—that is, to outlays for labor-power. He called the relation of constant to variable capital the *organic composition of capital.* The greater the ratio of constant to variable, the higher the composition. Under capitalism, the tendency was for the organic composition to rise—that is, for the constant to grow relative to the variable part, the latter growing only in absolute terms. Correspondingly, the *technical* composition of capital refers to the ratio of the mass of means of production to the mass of labor employed on them. The organic composition of capital refers both to the *value* ratio and the *technical* ratio; the two are strictly correlated. Because individual capitals vary in their organic composition, it is the average that Marx considers when he says that the ratio tends to rise historically.

from small, local to vast, worldwide markets. With each phase of this development, the average rate of profit varies. Primarily, it is the rising organic composition of capital that affects profits. The reader may recall that Marx's surplus-value theory argues that workers produce the value of their subsistence during one part of their working day and produce value over and above that quantity during the remainder of the working day. In *Capital*, Marx often assumed 100 percent to be the rate of surplus value $\left(\dfrac{s}{v}\right)$: that the workers produced the value of their subsistence during one half of the working day and that the capitalist appropriated the value of the other half of the day.

Now, if v stands for variable capital, c for constant capital, s for surplus value, and p' for rate of profit and we assume $\dfrac{s}{v}$ to be constant at 100 percent, we can employ Marx's (1962:207) hypothetical figures to illustrate how different rates of profit depend on different volumes of constant capital.

If $c = 50$, and $v = 100$, then $p' = 100/150 = 66\frac{2}{3}\%$
If $c = 100$, and $v = 100$, then $p' = 100/200 = 50\%$
If $c = 200$, and $v = 100$, then $p' = 100/300 = 33\frac{1}{3}\%$
If $c = 300$, and $v = 100$, then $p' = 100/400 = 25\%$
If $c = 400$, and $v = 100$, then $p' = 100/500 = 20\%$.

Marx (1962:207–08) explains:

> This is how the same rate of surplus-value would express itself under the same degree of labor exploitation in a falling rate of profit, because the material growth of the constant capital implies also a growth—albeit not in the same proportion—in its value, and consequently in that of the total capital.

If the changing composition of capital takes place in key spheres of production so that eventually it raises "the average organic composition of the total capital of a certain society, then the gradual growth of constant capital in relation to variable capital must necessarily lead to *a gradual fall of the general rate of profit,* so long as the rate of surplus-value, or the intensity of exploitation of labor by capital, remain the same" (Marx, 1962:208).

No paraphase could explain the significance of this as well as do Marx's (1962:208–09) own words. The rising organic composition of capital is

> just another expression for the progressive development of the social productivity of labor, which is demonstrated precisely by the fact that the same number of laborers, in the same time, i.e., with less labor, convert an ever increasing quantity of raw and auxiliary materials into products, thanks to the growing application of machinery and fixed capital in general. To this growing quantity of value of the constant capital . . . corresponds a progressive cheapening of products. Every individual product, considered by itself, contains a smaller quantity of labor than it did on a lower level of production, where the capital invested in wages occupies a far greater place compared to the capital invested in means of production. The hypothetical series drawn up at the beginning of this chapter expresses, therefore, the actual tendency of capitalist production. This mode of production produces a progressive relative decrease of the variable capital as compared to the constant capital, and consequently a continuously rising organic composition of the total capital. The immediate result of this is that the rate of surplus-value, at the same, or even a rising, degree of labor exploitation, is represented by a continuing falling general rate of profit. (We shall see later why this fall does not manifest itself in an absolute form, but rather as a tendency toward a progressive fall.)

How, according to Marx, does this law work itself out, and why not in an absolute form rather than as a tendency? What are the most important implications of this law?

Each capitalist seeks to obtain a larger share of the mass of surplus-value by intensifying the exploitation of labor and cutting his costs of production. The number of workers and the length and intensity of their labor are the variables that increase the mass of surplus-value. An increase in mass accompanied by a rise in the ratio of constant capital to the workers' wages can result in the expansion of the mass of surplus-value, and hence of profits, and yet be the consequence of a fall in the *rate* of profit.

If, again, we use Marx's (1962:213) hypothetical figures, this becomes quite evident:

$$\text{I.} \quad 4c + 2v + 2s; \; C = \;\; 6, \, p' = 33\tfrac{1}{3}\%$$
$$\text{II.} \quad 15c + 3v + 3s; \; C = 18, \, p' = 16\tfrac{2}{3}\%.$$

Here, we see clearly that while the mass of surplus value has increased by one-half, the rate of profit has fallen by one-half. The absolute magnitude of the profit has grown by 50 percent in spite of its enormous relative decrease compared to the total capital or the enormous decrease in the rate of profit. The number of workers employed by capital and the mass of surplus value produced by them

> can, consequently, increase, and increase progressively, in spite of the progressive drop in the rate of profit. And this not only *can* be so. Aside from the temporary fluctuations it *must* be so on the basis of capitalist production (Marx, 1962:213).

Of course, profits can decline both in rate and mass. This is what happened with the Great Crash of 1929 and the long depression that followed. We shall return to the phenomenon of economic crisis in a later context.

To understand better how the increase in the absolute mass of profit is accompanied by a declining rate of profit, we must recall the conditions of competitive capitalism. By striving to produce more profit, each business threatens the rate of profit of all. Each expands its equipment and tries to get its workers to convert as much raw material as possible in the shortest possible time into saleable commodities. To raise the productivity of labor, each competitor invests more and more in buildings and machines and purchases proportionately more raw material to be worked up in the accelerated production.

Thus, each capitalist, in seeking to reduce his costs per unit, contributes to the tendency toward a decline in the rate of profit of all which, in turn, further increases competition. To the extent that capitalists recognize this process, they intensify the exploitation of labor to the maximum possible, for this is one of the important means by which the tendential fall in the rate of profit can be temporarily averted and, in short periods of prosperity, even reversed. Under capitalism, this tendential law can be retarded and even pushed back for a time, but never can it be set aside. The temporary retarding and pushing back of the law are brought about by certain countertendencies.

COUNTERACTING INFLUENCES

Marx (1962:227–35) noted that if the rate of profit declines with the rising organic composition of capital, an "increasing intensity of exploitation" may counteract the tendential law. The labor-power purchased by variable capital may be exploited so intensely that it produces a rate of surplus-value that more than compensates for the declining rate of profit. Indeed, the rate of profit might even rise under these circumstances.

All capitalists try to reduce the costs of their products. This applies not only to consumers' goods manufacturers, but to producers' goods manufacturers as well. By reducing his costs, the manufacturer can reduce his prices to the capitalist who buys from him so that the increase in the value of constant capital is offset to the extent of that reduction. In addition, a reduction in the price of raw materials, as often occurs in times of crisis, temporarily reduces the proportion of constant capital required.

Other counteracting influences are the depression of wages below the value of labor-power and relative overpopulation—that is, the availability of abundant and cheap labor. Foreign trade may also make for another countertendency (as it frequently did while England enjoyed industrial hegemony). In Marx's (1962:232) view, because foreign trade "partly cheapens the elements of constant capital, and partly the necessities of life, for which the variable capital is exchanged, it tends to raise the rate of profit by increasing the rate of surplus-value and lowering the value of constant capital."

These counteracting influences accompany the further accumulation of capital, again causing variable capital to shrink in relation to constant capital and leading once more to a falling rate of profit. Marx (1962:233) believed that countertendencies

> do not do away with the law, but impair its effect.
> . . . Thus, the law acts only as a tendency. And it
> is only under certain circumstances and only after
> long periods that its effects become strikingly pronounced.

The most pronounced effects of this law and other contradictions of capitalism are expressed, according to Marx, in recurring and worsening economic crises.

2

Marx's Theory of Crisis

In his studies of the workings of capitalism, Marx never ceased to concern himself with the phenomenon of economic crisis, but he failed to develop a full and systematic theory of crisis. Neither in the three volumes of *Capital* nor in the three volumes of *Theories of Surplus-Value* is a thoroughly systematic treatment of the phenomenon to be found. As Paul Sweezy (1942:133–34) has observed, this is so partly because "crisis as a complex concrete phenomenon could not be fully analyzed on the levels of abstraction to which *Capital* is confined." Nevertheless, the main elements of a theory of crisis are to be found in *Capital*. Marxists have attempted to knit these elements into a coherent theory.[1] The discussion that follows presents the main outlines of that theory.

[1] Sweezy (1942) has made such an effort and has, in addition, provided a comprehensive account of the controversy on the nature of crisis. The reader should consult Sweezy's fine study, which I have relied on here and there.

Perhaps the best way to begin is to bring into re\
the nature of capitalist crises by contrasting them wi ..
crises of the precapitalist era. The typical crisis of precapitalist economies was one in which production failed to
meet the needs of the people. Whether this condition was
the result of natural disaster, war, poor harvest, or other
causes, production was deficient and caused great suffering
among the poor. People were starving, but the warehouses
were not bulging with food and other commodities that
could not be sold at a profit. Under capitalism, the situation
has been just the reverse. The recurrent problem is overproduction and the declining ability of the people to consume what they have produced. — ie E.E.c food mountains,
    The history of capitalism revealed this tendency: a
period of growth of the productive forces is followed by a
period of severe disruption. A portion of the commodities
produced finds no market, production declines, unemployment rises, and profits and wages drop. This condition prevails for periods of varying duration, after which production again begins to rise and the unemployed are brought
back into production that not only attains the highest level
of the preceding period, but eventually surpasses it.
    Interpretations of such crises have been numerous.
Basically, they fall into two categories that one might label
for convenience non-Marxian and Marxian. The non-Marxian view has been that crises are mere disturbances; they
are temporary interruptions of production that probably
are avoidable. In contrast, Marxists have regarded crises as
manifestations of the fundamental contradictions of capitalism. Crises are inherent in the capitalist economic system;
not only are they unavoidable, but will become progressively
more severe until they have discredited capitalism in the
eyes of the people.
    Recalling our earlier discussion of the accumulation
and concentration of capital, its rising organic composition,
and the tendential law of falling rate of profit, we begin to
see the main elements of Marx's conception of the causes of
crisis.
    The primary motive and purpose of capitalist produc-

tion is to realize surplus-value or to convert it into profits. In the actual process of production, capital absorbs a certain quantity of surplus-value or unpaid labor. But in order to convert this quantity into profit, Marx (1962:239) writes,

> The entire mass of commodities, i.e., the total product, including the portion which replaces the constant and variable capital, and that representing surplus-value, must be sold. If this is not done, or done only in part, or only at prices below the prices of production, the laborer has been indeed exploited, but his exploitation is not realized as such for the capitalist, and this can be bound up with a total or partial failure to realize the surplus-value pressed out of him, indeed even with the partial or total loss of the capital. The conditions of direct exploitation, and those of realizing it, are not identical.

Continuing this line of reasoning, Marx (1962:239) argues that the realization of surplus-value is determined by the sale of the commodities which, in turn, is determined not by the "absolute consumer power, but by the consumer power based on antagonistic conditions of distribution, which reduce the consumption of the bulk of society to a minimum varying within more or less narrow limits."

The growth of the productive forces results in an ever greater mass of commodities. Under capitalism, however, there is nothing to guarantee that the market will grow apace. On the contrary, according to Marx (240), conditions regulating the market "assume more and more the form of a natural law working independently of the producer, and become ever more uncontrollable."

The periodic results of this conflict between the growing productive forces and the existing property relations are crises that Marx (1962:244) says "are always but momentary and forcible solutions of the existing contradictions. They are violent eruptions which for a time restore the disturbed equilibrium. [In these terms, the] *real barrier* of capitalist production is *capital itself*." The limits imposed by the inability of the great mass of producers to consume what they have produced, Marx (1962:245) continues, "come continually into conflict with the methods of production employed by capital for its purposes, which drive towards unlimited extension of production, towards production as an end in itself, towards unconditional development of the social productivity of labor."

How is the conflict settled? By periodically withdrawing or partially destroying the excess capital. Equilibrium soon is restored and the cycle begins anew. Ultimately, the root cause of these crises, for Marx (1962:251), is that a "rift must continually ensue between the limited dimensions of consumption under capitalism and a production which forever tends to exceed this immanent barrier." Because capitalists produce for profit rather than to meet the needs of the people and the people have needs but often without "effective demand," this result is inevitable under capitalism.

It follows that crises are *not* caused by the production of too many necessaries of life in proportion to the existing population. Quite the reverse. Production reaches a comparative standstill because more means of production and subsistence have been produced than can serve as means for the exploitation of laborers at a certain rate of profit. For Marx (253), the point is not that "too much wealth is produced. But [that] at times too much wealth is produced in its capitalistic, self-contradictory forms."

Under capitalism, then, it is precisely the development of the productive forces, and the accompanying tendency toward a falling rate of profit that periodically create a conflict with that very development—a conflict that can be overcome only through crisis. Expansion, contraction, and renewed expansion are determined

> by profit and the proportion of this profit to the employed capital, thus by a definite rate of profit, rather than the relation of production to social requirements, i.e., to the requirements of socially developed human beings. It is for this reason that the capitalist mode of production meets with barriers at a certain expanded stage of production

which, if viewed from the other premise, would
. . . have been altogether inadequate. It [produc-
tion] comes to a standstill at a point fixed by the
production and realization of profit, and not the
satisfaction of [human] requirements (253).

We see, then, that for Marx, crises occur because capitalists must expand the productive forces but consumption
cannot keep apace. This is so because the property relations
(often referred to as class structure) of capitalist society
imposed rather narrow limits on the "effective demand,"
to use the Keynesian phrase, of the bulk of the people. Some
Marxists have called this the "underconsumption" theory
of crisis.[2]

Yet the actual process leading to crisis entails additional complexities. Although Marx did not work it out in
detail, his conception of crisis as arising out of underconsumption allows for disproportionality as a contributing
and aggravating factor. This deserves brief elaboration.

It is mainly in the second volume of *Capital* that Marx
discusses the two departments of production: *production of
the means of production* and *production of the means of
consumption*. The greater the development of capitalism, the
greater the proportion of means of production in total production. Because workers purchase means of consumption
or subsistence with their wages, these goods normally are
disposed of without excessive difficulty. Disposing of the
means of production, however, eventually becomes quite
difficult and, for a time, even impossible.

Producers' goods such as machines are produced to
meet the demands of capitalists to expand production. As
a result, these goods are at first easily disposed of. Expansion of the market for producers' goods is accompanied by
a concomitant expansion of the market for consumers' goods.
The reason for this is that additional workers are needed
for the expanded production and their wages increase the
sale of consumers' goods.

[2] See Sweezy (1942:156 *ff.*) for a comparison of this theory
with another arguing that crises arise from "disproportionality."

During this period of expansion, markets are therefore readily available. Soon, however, expansion ends and the construction of factories and the manufacturing of machines comes to a halt. The workers who built the factories and manufactured the machines are laid off. As a result, the laid-off workers who remain unemployed no longer have money with which to purchase consumers' goods or their purchasing power diminishes significantly. While consumption is thus diminishing, the production of consumer goods continues to expand because of the enlarged productive capacity provided by the new producers' goods. A crisis is the result.

Thus, expansion of production and prosperity are followed by a crisis in which the uncompetitive capitalists fall by the wayside; but the new levels of productivity and the new price levels make a renewed expansion possible for those capitalists who survived the storm.

Falling prices and competitive struggle constrain every capitalist to lower the costs of his total product below the general level by means of new machines and productive methods. Each strives to increase the productivity of labor —that is, to decrease the proportion of variable to constant capital—and thereby dispense with some workers. In Marx's (1962:250) words, eventually, "depreciation of the elements of constant capital would itself tend to raise the rate of profit. The mass of employed constant capital would have increased in relation to variable, but its value could have fallen." In this way, temporary stagnation prepared the way for the expansion of production.

For Marx, then, to say that crises result not from underconsumption but from a disproportion between the two main departments of production clearly was a pseudo-explanation. Disproportionality is a dimension of the general process leading to "overproduction" under capitalism. Inevitably, the process manifests itself as long as "production imposes itself as a blind law upon the agents of production, and not as a law which, being understood and hence controlled by their common mind, brings the productive process under their joint control" (Marx, 1962:251–52).

It becomes clear, even from these rudiments of a theory, that without new markets, capitalism could not overcome its crises. To understand how capitalism found and created these markets, we must review the historical conditions in which capitalism emerged and developed as a social, economic, and political system.[3]

THE DEVELOPMENT OF THE CAPITALIST MODE OF PRODUCTION

Apparently, Marx's belief that he was living in an age of mature and even senescent capitalism ready for transformation into socialism was one of his principal errors. Hindsight enables us to perceive that actually, the capitalism he was studying was young and virile and in the early stages of an economic system that was to reveal remarkable capacities for further development and extension.

Marx understood that the capitalism of his time was expanding at the expense of precapitalist forms of production, thus creating two auxiliary bodies of the industrial reserve army whose origins he described quite accurately. The first was created by mass migration from the countryside to the towns. The second was composed of formerly independent craftsmen who had been unable to compete with modern industry and joined the ranks of those seeking industrial employment. The existence of an inordinately large industrial reserve army led to a situation in which living standards (real wages) remained almost stagnant. As Sternberg (1946:23) notes, the first half of the nineteenth century

was the one which provided Marx with the empirical material for his analysis of unemployment and economic crises; it is therefore not surprising that on this basis he confidently expected a further

[3] A superb treatment of this problem may be found in Fritz Sternberg (1946). In this review, I rely heavily on Sternberg's work.

sharp intensification of social conflicts even for
this early stage of capitalist development.

Beginning in mid-nineteenth century, a pronounced
change is apparent. This is the time at which Britain and
other European nations were extending their sway throughout the world. Results of British rule in India illustrate the
effects of territorial expansion during this period. British
large-scale industry dumped large quantities of cheap goods
on the Indian market, thereby forcing a multitude of small
independent craftsmen out of it. This process was similar
to the course of events that had occurred earlier in Europe,
but with one important difference: the European craftsman
defeated by capitalist competition eventually found employment in the developing industrial system, but his Indian
counterpart could not.

Development of a native industrial capitalism in India
was not conducive to the interest of British imperialism.
British rulers, therefore, actively sought to prevent its development and, in fact, succeeded in doing so. As a result,
British industry, particularly textiles, was able to employ
an increasing number of British workers in spite of the
growing mechanization of production. The destruction of a
large portion of the Indian weaving industry and the fore-
stalled development of a large industrial working class
provided an extended market for British goods and enabled
British industry to employ many more workers than otherwise would have been possible.

But another important factor contributed to the allevi-
ation of crises in Europe during the second half of the nineteenth century: mass migration from Europe to the United
States. Peasants, unemployed workers, and supplanted
craftsmen poured across the sea, thus markedly reducing
the industrial reserve army and alleviating the social antagonisms of Europe. For these reasons and others, the
growth of capitalism from approximately 1850 to 1913 was
characterized by an absolute increase in the work force of
millions of workers and a marked rise in real wages and the
standard of living. Sternberg (1946:25) observed that if we

take the level of wages in 1913 as 100, then wages in Great Britain stood at 57 in 1850, but by 1855 they had risen to 63, and increases, with setbacks, followed until the end of the century: 1860, 64; 1865, 67; 1870, 70; 1875, 89; 1880, 81; 1885, 82; 1890, 90; 1895, 88; and 1900, 100.

As the result of a variety of factors, capitalism enlarged its orbit and gained new markets, *apparently* overcoming some of its contradictions. The following five factors appear to have been the most important:

1. Expansion of British and, to a lesser extent, French capitalism at the expense of precapitalist forms, both at home and abroad in the colonies each had established;

2. Growth of capitalism in other European countries from its infancy until it became the dominant mode of production (as in Germany);

3. Extension of capitalism into politically sovereign but relatively undeveloped countries (such as in Russia and Japan);

4. Phenomenal growth of capitalism in the United States, Canada, and in other British Dominions—areas that enabled European capitalism to export staggering amounts of capital and other goods and to disencumber itself of many millions of Europe's inhabitants; finally,

5. European capitalism's domination of the many areas of Asia and Africa enabled the mother countries to decide in their own interests what aspects of the dominated economies should be developed and how this development should be accomplished.

As a result of these historical developments, capitalism seemed to exhibit characteristics that Marxists had considered impossible. Instead of progressive unemployment and impoverishment or earnings stabilized at a low level, employment was growing and the standard of living was rising. Although crises continued to occur during this period, they were overcome with relative ease. Production and foreign trade increased, while wages and profits rose. Little wonder, then, that economists and other students of capitalism became convinced that the Marxian theory of recurrent and worsening crises had been refuted effectively. In this regard, Sternberg (1946:26) cites the well-known German economist, Werner Sombart:

> Marx developed his crisis theory, at a time when England in particular was being visited by a very severe "crisis," which also affected the continent, and it was therefore not unreasonable to adopt the idea that the setbacks which followed on periods of progress would become more and more severe. The line of development of 1825, 1836, and 1847 could be continued, and then the theory of catastrophe developed by Marx seemed feasible. . . . The crisis of 1857 was the last large-scale catastrophe England experienced. Germany and Austria suffered a severe crisis in 1873, but since then there is a clear tendency in European economic life for antagonistic features to balance each other, to grow less serious, and finally to disappear altogether, a tendency which continued until the World War and which was not weakened by the war and what followed or turned into its opposite.

Continuing, Sternberg (1946:26) observes: "Werner Sombart wrote this in 1928. One year later we had the worst crisis in the history of capitalism." Fritz Sternberg and other Marxists argue convincingly that the capitalist world never really overcame the great crisis that began in 1929.

3

The Crisis of 1929

The tremendous expansion of capitalism that began around 1850 and ended with the close of World War I occurred at a time when only ten or twenty percent of the world's inhabitants lived and produced under capitalistic conditions. Given this limited orbit of the capitalist system, every small expansion into noncapitalist areas reacted as a favorable stimulus on the capitalist centers.

In contrast, the period between the end of World War I and the Great Crash was one in which capitalism had drawn nearly half the world's population into its sphere of influence. Sternberg (1946:28) concluded that under these circumstances, the "expansion and conquest of new markets would have to proceed on a really tremendous scale to produce even the same effects as were formerly obtained by comparatively modest expansion into relatively small areas." However, the facts indicate that far from a tremendous expansion, hardly any new markets at all were opened. Indeed, expansion was less than it had been during the last decade

before World War I. At the same time, the number of capitalist countries seeking new markets increased. Of these,
the position of the United States had changed radically as
compared with its position during the preceding period.

During the nineteenth century, the United States not
only absorbed much of Europe's "surplus population," but
also provided European capitalists with great opportunities
for investment and growing markets for their industries. In
the same period, the United States itself extended the
sway of capitalism over most of its territory.

Between the two world wars, however, the United
States changed its fundamental position and closed its gates
to large-scale European immigration. Eventually, Canada
followed suit. No longer could the United States be counted
on to alleviate European problems of unemployment by absorbing a substantial portion of Europe's industrial reserve
army. In addition, United States had transformed itself
from a predominantly agrarian and weak industrial society
into the most powerful industrial country in the world. At
the same time, it declined as a market for European industrial goods and capital investment.

By now, the United States had fully extended capitalism
within its own boundaries. Internal markets alone were no
longer sufficient: she began to develop trade with countries
in Asia and Latin America. Not only had the United States
decreased her importation of European capital to a small
fraction of what it had been, but also she became the largest
exporter of capital in the world. In short, the United States
had become a powerful capitalist state seeking new markets
outside its boundaries. Changes in the situation of the
United States served to exacerbate the already intense social
conflicts in Europe, and in the United States itself, problems
and conflicts associated with industrial capitalism were becoming ever more evident.

At roughly the same time, Japan also emerged as a vigorous capitalist industrial power. Not only had she successfully maintained her political sovereignty, but now she
entered the competition for new markets on the Asiatic
mainland. Proximity of the markets together with coopera-

tion and support of the government gave Japanese capitalism definite advantages. Entrance of these two rapidly industrializing powerful capitalist nations into the competition for markets contributed significantly to aggravation of the problems and conflicts of European capitalism. Nevertheless, this change was not the decisive factor. More important was the fact that during the interval between World War I and World War II, the arena in which the struggle for markets had been waged actually contracted.

Before World War I, Russia's role in European capitalism had become increasingly significant. By providing a growing market for industrial products, Russia helped European industries increase production and employ larger numbers of workers. The Bolshevik revolution put an end to this role once and for all. Sternberg (1946) notes that between 1919 and 1929, not once did trade between the Soviet Union and the rest of Europe attain the prewar level.

Another factor contributing to the great crisis that began in 1929 was the situation in the noncapitalist world. Almost half of the world's population lived in Asia and Africa—an immense potential market—but the policies of such imperialist nations as Britain, France, and Holland precluded full development of these markets. This may be best illustrated by the British policy in India.

In the years between 1900 and 1913, India had served as a continually expanding market for British industrial goods. While the total value of India's foreign trade had grown by approximately 150 percent, its railway network

> increased from about 25,000 miles to about 35,000 miles, or by 40%. The total tonnage carried in 1900–01 was 44 millions, while in 1913–14 it had almost doubled and amounted to 84 millions. From the beginning of the twentieth century up to the First World War the production of coal in India increased from 6,217,000 tons to 16,468,000 tons, or by about 150% (Sternberg, 1946:33).

In spite of these substantial increases, India remained a predominantly agrarian economy. In India, the British pursued a policy calculated to develop only those sectors of the economy that suited British interests and to prevent general and systematic industrialization. India imported no less than 64.2 percent of its goods from England. There is therefore no doubt that during this period especially, limited and one-sided industrialization of India created enormous markets for British imperialism, not to mention the great wealth derived from systematic exploitation of hundreds of millions of natives.

Ironically, this very limited and selective industrialization of India was precisely the element that soon began to have constricting effects on the British economy. Sternberg (1946:33) observed that

> For India to have continued to play the role of an expanding market for Great Britain, and for the world capitalist system in the period between the two world wars, a very considerable increase in the industrialization of the country would have been necessary, coupled with a rise in the living standard of the Indian people; a process in which Great Britain and the rest of the world could have participated. However, nothing of the sort occurred.

India remained industrially stagnant. From 1920 to 1929, her industrial work force increased only by some 300,000. This stagnation also expressed itself in the volume of India's foreign trade which "was no greater in 1929 than it had been in 1913. Thus India had ceased to function in this period as an ever-growing market for the industrial exports of imperialism, though its role as an old market was more or less maintained" (Sternberg, 1946:34).

Slow and selective industrialization was characteristic of all colonies of European imperialism, as it was of other precapitalist areas such as China. A number of imperialist powers, including Britain, France, Japan, Germany, and the United States, vied for advantageous positions from which to exploit China's resources. These powers wanted markets, sources of cheap raw material for their industries, and cheap labor. They were not interested in the industrialization of China for the same reasons that they were not interested in the industrialization of their colonies—reasons that will become clearer in a later systematic discussion of imperialism. For now, it is sufficient to emphasize that not only did China remain economically undeveloped, but that whatever modern industries she had were owned and controlled by foreign interests.

In India and China and throughout the colonial areas of Asia, Africa, and Latin America, industrialization was fostered only to a point and in limited forms. This limitation is an important factor in accounting for the abrupt stop in the process of dynamic expansion that began in 1850 and transformed capitalism into a dominant mode of production.

To summarize, a combination of the following three conditions appear to have constricted the economies of the most advanced capitalist countries of the time severely:

1. Emergence of new capitalist powers and their entry into the competition for markets;
2. The Russian Revolution of 1917, which removed or substantially lessened the role of that vast land as a market; and
3. Extreme retardation and one-sided development of the colonial and semicolonial areas of the world.

These conditions resulted in a stagnation in 1929 of the volume of foreign trade between the colonial and semicolonial areas and the advanced industrial countries at the 1913 level or thereabouts.

INCREASING UNEMPLOYMENT IN THE YEARS BEFORE THE CRISIS

Although the conditions we have just described were developing throughout the 1920s, their constricting effects were not felt immediately. The destruction caused by World War

I, the reduced productive capacity, and the backlog of demand conduced to a few years of growth after the war. Soon, however, expansion of the productive apparatus ceased, resulting in unutilized productive capacity and large numbers of unemployed—more than a million in all of the advanced capitalist countries.

In Germany, unemployment rose from 911,000 in 1924 to 1,353,000 in 1928; Sternberg (1946:46) concluded that in Britain, unemployment was "greater than in the decade before the First World War, and greater than at any time during the second half of the nineteenth century"; and although he lacked reliable unemployment statistics for the United States, Sternberg showed that with the great increase in labor productivity from 1919 to 1929, no increase in the number of workers was required to produce a much larger volume of commodities.

This means that even during the period of *prosperity* preceding the crash, unemployment was high throughout the capitalist world—higher, often, than it had been during previous crises. The fact that this was universally true indicates that some general cause was at work: contraction of old markets and relative unavailability of new ones at a time when the total productive capacity of capitalism had increased immensely. The result: a crisis of unprecedented severity and scope.

Available data show just how great was the decline in world production from 1929 to 1932. Excluding the Soviet Union, world industrial production dropped to 63.8 percent of its 1929 level—that is, by more than a third.

The decline in world production was accompanied by a rise in unemployment; at the depth of the Depression, some 30 million workers were unemployed. This figure is surely conservative, for it "does not include workers on short time, or 'invisible' unemployment. If these two items are added the total would certainly exceed forty millions." (Woytinskii, 1936:142–3; cited in Sternberg, 1946:44–45.) Finally, there was a disastrous decline in the volume of world trade: "If we take 1929 at 100 then it declined, according to the statistics of the League of Nations, to 74. In no previous crisis in the history of capitalism was there even remotely any such drop" (Sternberg, 1946:44).

UNIVERSAL EFFECTS OF THE CRISIS

The crisis that began in 1929 was unprecedented in still other respects. It went deeper than any previous crisis and was more extensive, both geographically and socially. It struck all capitalist countries, old and new, the colonial areas as well as the mother capitalist countries. Moreover, all social classes were affected—in sharp contrast to previous crises that had affected capitalists and workers, but not peasants, farmers, pensioners and officials. Some classes and groups had weathered previous crises and even improved their living standards as the result of the stability of their monetary incomes at a time when prices were dropping. "The fact that there was an economic area within capitalist society which was immune from the effects of the crisis" Sternberg (1946:46) convincingly observes "naturally facilitated the overcoming of the crisis itself. During the 1929 crisis there was no such immune sector under capitalism anywhere."

The vulnerability of all groups and classes was also a consequence of the fact that the crisis of 1929 was agricultural as well as industrial. Clearly, as long as precapitalist forms of agricultural production prevailed and peasants were not heavily dependent on the capitalist market, its vicissitudes had little effect on the peasantry. Correspondingly, the methods of production in the countryside were not likely to result in "overproduction" in agriculture. However, in light of the marked capitalization and mechanization of agriculture throughout the capitalist world in the decades prior to the Crash, it is not difficult to understand why agriculture was so severely affected. Improved methods yielded a great volume of produce for which no market was readily available, and this at a time when farmers and peasants increasingly depended on the market for money income to meet their rent, tax, and other financial obligations.

The 1929 crisis was therefore truly universal: it was worldwide and it affected all sectors of the economy and all classes of the society. As we shall see, one must seriously question whether this crisis actually was overcome, as some of the conditions that prevailed before and during the crisis (namely, the small number of opening new markets) continued to prevail right up to the beginning of World War II. In these terms, the crisis of 1929 was universal and more. In Sternberg's (1946) words, it was also an "unliquidated crisis" because there were no new markets with which to liquidate it. This is apparent from a brief review of the situation in the period between the crisis and World War II.

The Soviet Union failed to provide an expanded market for capitalism; quite to the contrary, it provided a substantially contracted one. In 1938, one year before the outbreak of World War II, the Soviet Union's foreign trade totaled only a quarter of the total reached by Czarist Russia in 1913.

Between 1920 and 1929, immigration to the United States was cut to half of the 1905–14 total, and it continued to decline until the period 1935–39, when it reached the low of 272,422. Total immigration during the decade 1929–39 "was less than the total of any single year in the period 1904–14" (Sternberg, 1946:52). So the United States contributed nothing to the relief of unemployment in Europe. Indeed, the fall in the level of U.S. production and trade was worse than that of Europe's. Suffering great losses in their export capital, American businessmen not only failed to export new capital, but even withdrew much of the old.

Furthermore, the markets and natural resources of the new states that had emerged in central Europe soon became the exclusive preserve of Nazi Germany. We have already noted that as a result of the policy of European imperialism, the various colonial and neocolonial areas remained after 1929 as industrially stagnant as before, thus providing no new markets that might have contributed to the liquidation of the crisis.

Finally, Japan's state capitalism and militarized economy enabled her to escape the worst effects of the crisis, thereby intensifying these effects on the other capitalist nations. Japan almost monopolized foreign trade through her empire and the other areas under her control. Her share of world trade even increased somewhat during this period, in sharp contrast to the situation of European capitalism. For all these reasons, "world capitalism entered the Second World War in a state of latent crisis" (Sternberg, 1946:54). Table 1 readily shows the truth of this assertion.

Clearly, only in one year did world capitalist production surpass the 1929 level. In fact, these figures tend to underestimate the decline because they include the increased production for purposes of war of Germany and Japan as well as of Great Britain, France, and others. Figures for nonmilitary production alone would show the disparity to be even greater. This difference is illustrated in Table 2 by comparing the production statistics of the United States, where production for military purposes was at a minimum during this period, with those of Germany, where armament production had become substantial.

These figures clearly show that U.S. production failed to attain the 1929 level before World War II. This was an unprecedented phenomenon. Never before had production failed to attain the pre-crisis level of prosperity within the decade after the crisis. As for Germany, data show the

TABLE 1

Index of World Production in the Mining and
Manufacturing Industries (Excluding USSR)

	Index
1934	77.7*
1935	86.0
1936	96.4
1937	103.7
1938	93.0

Source: *Statistical Yearbook of the League
of Nations, 1938-39*, pp. 180–81.
    * 1929 production = 100.

TABLE 2

Index of Industrial Production in the United States
and Germany

	U.S.	Germany
1934	66.4*	79.8*
1935	75.6	94.0
1936	88.1	106.3
1937	92.2	117.2
1938	72.3	126.2

Source: *Statistical Yearbook of the League of Nations, 1938–39*, pp. 180–181.
* 1929 production = 100.

extent to which German economic recovery was attributable
to Nazi production for war—production on a scale unprecedented in capitalist countries during peacetime.

Now let us look at the figures for other major capitalist
countries as shown in Table 3. We see that neither in France
nor in Italy did production again attain the 1929 level; in
the case of Italy, this was true in spite of her considerable
increase in production for war. British production did rise
but, as Sternberg explains, special factors were at work:
Britain's 1929 production was relatively low—in fact, below

TABLE 3

Index of Industrial Production in the United Kingdom,
France, Italy, and Japan

	U.K.	France	Italy	Japan
1934	98.6*	75.2*	80.0*	128.7*
1935	105.6	72.5	93.8	141.8
1936	115.8	78	87.5	151.1
1937	123.6	81.7	99.6	170.8
1938	115.5	76.1	98.5	173.0

Source: *Statistical Yearbook of the League of Nations, 1938–39*, pp. 80–81.
* 1929 production = 100.

the level of 1913. In addition, her crisis was somewhat less severe than those of other countries because the decline in import prices of food and raw materials was far greater than was the decline in export prices, "two-thirds of which consisted of manufactured products. The close relationship between Great Britain and her colonies also played an important role; so did the increase in armament production, though, of course, to nothing like the same extent as in Germany" (Sternberg, 1946:56–57).

Japan was the only capitalist country other than Germany that exhibited a phenomenal increase in production over the 1929 level. The reasons for this are easy to grasp. Japan already had embarked on a large-scale militarization program and had invaded Manchuria in 1931, thereby grabbing new markets for herself. Yet, in spite of both Germany's and Japan's marked increases resulting from war production and in spite of the increased military production of Britain, France and others (although substantially smaller than that of Nazi Germany), *world* industrial production, excluding the USSR remained well below the pre-crisis level of 1929.

At the same time, millions of workers were permanently unemployed throughout the capitalist world. Until the outbreak of World War II, unemployment exceeded the 1929 level. Even in Great Britain where production figures exceeded the 1929 level, unemployment remained exceptionally high—10.3 percent in 1938.

As for the United States, the unemployment level in 1939 reached 10.4 millions, almost 20 percent of the total labor force.

Similarly, world trade had sunk precipitously after 1929. Although there was a slight recovery in 1937, both world industrial production and world trade fell again in 1938. Unlike any other capitalist crisis, this one had persisted for almost a full decade and recovery was still a goal; both industry and agriculture remained in a state of depression. For example, at the outset of World War II, agriculture had not yet recovered from its prolonged and serious crisis. The United States and other capitalist countries entered World War II without having overcome the most profound and widespread crisis of capitalism's history.

During and after World War II, capitalism appeared once again to have immunized itself against economic crisis. Yet there have been in the United States, for example, several recessions since the end of the war. The first occurred just before the outbreak of the Korean conflict in 1950 and, most recently, at the time of this writing (1971), we are experiencing a simultaneous inflation and recession with considerable unemployment among both unskilled and highly skilled workers—including highly educated technicians, scientists, and other professionals with PhD degrees. This situation persists in spite of annual astronomic allocations for military purposes.

The need for research in and answers to questions such as the following is apparent: Is there still at work in present-day capitalist-industrial society a tendency toward crisis? If so, what are the sources of this tendency? What are some of the countertendencies that appear to be at work? How might these conflicting tendencies resolve themselves?

To provide even the merest beginnings of an adequate answer to these complex and fateful questions, the structure of contemporary capitalism must be studied to see how it compares and contrasts with the capitalism of Marx's time. This means that we shall have to examine what Marxists call the monopoly stage of capitalism and its corresponding foreign policy of imperialist expansion and domination.

As we saw earlier, Marx recognized and analyzed the powerful tendency toward the concentration and centralization of capital. And of course Lenin, to whom we shall return in due course, regarded imperialism as the highest stage of capitalism and he intimately associated the formation of monopolies with the concentration of production.

When Marxists speak of "monopoly," they do not necessarily mean that a single party, corporation, or group exclusively owns and controls the production and distribution of a given commodity or commodities. Rather, they use the term to refer to the powerful tendency toward the concentration of economic power in the hands of a few corporate giants who implicitly or explicitly exercise control over whole industries and, in effect, wield monopoly power. Nonetheless, the term "monopoly capital" may grate on the ears of some readers. I therefore use the term "corporate capitalism" instead, as both non-Marxists and Marxists agree that the major organizational structure and agency of present-day capital is the giant corporation. Bear in mind, however, that when one speaks of monopoly power, this is no mere phrase-mongering.

Baran and Sweezy (1966:51) have acknowledged that "today there are probably fewer genuine monopolies [in the United States] than there were at the turn of the century." Nevertheless, the fundamental differences between competitive capitalism and the capitalism of today should not be obscured. One need not be a Marxist to recognize them. For example, Stocking and Watson (1950:82) have observed:

> The merging of business competitors need not go so far as complete unification, 100 percent monopoly, to reduce competitive pressures—and yield extra profits. Power to restrict supply and raise prices need not be absolute to be worthwhile. It helps to ensure profits if the number of sellers is so small that each will recognize the benefits of following a live-and-let-live policy.

And A. A. Berle (1954:17) writes:

> The impact of many corporations—for example, General Motors, or the great oil companies—goes beyond the confines of their actual ownership. For example, at a rough estimate, some three billions of dollars are invested in garages and facilities owned by so-called "small" businessmen who hold agency contracts from the principal automobile manufacturers. The owners are small, independent businessmen usually trading as "corporations" but certainly not giants. They are, nominally, independent. But their policies, operations, and, in a large measure, their prices, are determined by the motor company whose cars they sell.

The same is true of the "small businessman" who "owns" a gasoline-filling station. The ability of the large corporation to make decisions and direct operations overflows the area of its ownership.

A better appreciation of what is meant by monopoly capital and the basic difference between monopoly and the competitive stage of capitalism can be gained by a brief exploration of the transition from one to the other.

4

The Second Industrial Revolution

The term "second industrial revolution" generally refers to several pronounced technological changes of the late nineteenth century that resulted in new sources of power and higher productivity in industry. Oil and electricity now joined coal; the gas engine and electric motor increasingly replaced steam as sources of industrial power. Steel became a basic industrial material, having received a new impetus from the "introduction of the Bessemer process, the open-hearth furnace, and the Siemens-Martin regenerators, together with processes for hardening steel with alloys" (Mandel, 1968:393).[1]

The important point to note for our purposes is that this technical and industrial revolution greatly accelerated the process of concentration and centralization of capital.

[1] The present discussion is based on Ernest Mandel (1968).

One reason for this is that the new technology in steel, aluminum, electricity, and so forth was used in highly expensive, large-scale capital equipment. The growing cost of the immense minimum appartus required to enter profitable production conduced to a situation in which new industries became the preserve of big concerns. In the words of Fritz Machlup (1952:123), the enormous costs of fixed capital and other initial investments generally acted as "a sort of 'natural barrier to entry.'"

However, another important reason for the accelerated concentration was the fact that the main *locus* of the "second industrial revolution" was not England, but the United States, Germany, Japan, and, to a lesser extent, Russia and Italy. These countries, the so-called latecomers, did not have to begin where the "first arrivals"—Britain, France, and Belgium—had begun a century or so earlier. They did not have to recapitulate all the stages of industrial development in England, for example.

In this sense, the latecomers enjoyed a considerable advantage. They could begin at the most advanced and modern stage and embark on rapid industrialization at the point at which the organic composition of capital was highest and concentration most pronounced. This meant that they were relatively less encumbered than were the first arrivals by a productive plant with a lower organic composition of capital. As a result they were more vigorous than the earlier entrants had been from a strictly economic standpoint, but they found most of the existing world market under the control of the first arrivals—an important point to which we shall return in our discussion of imperialism.

Accentuated concentration was therefore most marked among the latecomers. Big enterprises in those countries employed a growing proportion of the labor force. In Germany, for example, enterprises employing 200 employees or more increased from 11.9 percent in 1882 to 45.1 percent in 1961 (in the German Federal Republic). In 1961, 2 percent of the employees in Germany (GFR) were employed in enterprises with fewer than 10 employees; in 1882, nearly two-thirds had been thus employed.

As for the United States, the number of manufacturing establishments employing over 1,000 employees increased "from 540 in 1909 to 21,106 in 1955" (Mandel, 1968:396). Enterprises employing *fewer* than 500 people declined from 72 percent of all employees in 1909 to 54.3 percent in 1955. And if, on the other hand, we take a look at enterprises employing *more* than 1,000 people, we find that these employed 15.3 percent of all employees in 1909; 17.4 percent in 1914; 24.2 percent in 1929; and 33.6 percent in 1955.

According to Mandel's (1968:397) data, "the *average* size of manufacturing enterprises increased from 8 employees in 1850, 9 in 1860, and 10.5 in 1880 to 35 in 1914, 40 in 1929, 53 in 1939 and 55.4 in 1954. In the last mentioned year, enterprises with over 1,000 employees concentrated 32.8 percent of the total personnel employed in industry, but produced 37 percent of the 'value added' in industry."

Incomes and profits are even more concentrated than is labor. Thus, the Department of Internal Revenue's data show that companies with net annual revenue exceeding five million dollars increased from 34.17 percent in 1918 to 50.69 percent in 1942. Mandel (1968:398) reported that while data of the Federal Trade Commission indicate that "the 200 largest companies in the United States had 35 percent of the turnover of all companies in 1935, 37 percent in 1947, 40.5 percent in 1950 and 47 percent in 1958. The postwar boom, which saw the number of manufacturing companies increase by 50 percent, thus did not bring a fall-off in concentration. On the contrary, this continued vigorously, but the number of very large enterprises which emerged from this concentration evidently increased in a period of lively expansion."

The higher organic composition of capital together with its accelerated concentration, the major technical advances of the turn of the century, and the immense capital investment required for production are factors that contributed to the process in which a relatively small number of manufacturers acquired control of industries as well as large shares of the market at the expense of small- and middle-sized producers.

But the largest enterprises also encountered risks. Their immense capital investments required a comparatively rapid amortization. Price competition leads to a falling rate of profit that can prove mutually disadvantageous and even disastrous; as the results of this reality soon became apparent, the giants of industry quickly arrived at understandings and agreements that precluded price competition. Their control of supply and prices and, hence, profits was concerted and effective.

There are innumerable examples that would illustrate this strategy, but one will suffice. Mandel (1968:399) quotes from an interview of H. H. Rogers, a Rockefeller associate who had participated in forming the Standard Oil Trust, by the *New York Tribune* in 1874:

> If by common consent, in good faith, the refiners agree to reduce the quantities to an allotment for each, made in view of the supply and demand, and the capacity for production, the market can be regulated with a reasonable profit for all. The price of oil today is fifteen cents per gallon. The proposed allotment of business would probably advance the price to twenty cents. . . . Oil to yield a fair profit should be sold for twenty-five cents per gallon.

Understandings, alliances, agreements, combines, cartels, and so forth soon were arrived at not only in the same industry and in the same country, but internationally as well.

High capital concentration in industry made such oligopolistic and even monopolistic control possible. Earlier, under competitive capitalism, enterprises in a given industry were too numerous to organize into an effective monopoly. A small new capital was sufficient to break it up. Later, however, with the high concentration and domination by a few giant firms of whole branches of industry, objective conditions became much more favorable for the effective organization of monopoly control.

The "second industrial revolution" and its concomitant developments occurred mainly among the latecomers—the

U.S.A., Germany, and Japan. As might be expected, monopolies also emerged in those countries first and, of course, in the new industries such as oil, steel, automobiles, electric apparatuses, chemicals, and so on.

The trend with which Americans probably are most familiar is the progressive decline in the number of automobile-producing companies from 265 in 1909 to 88 in 1921, 44 in 1926, 11 in 1937, and 6 in 1955. Today, as we know, there are two supergiants (General Motors and Ford), one giant (Chrysler), and one minigiant (American Motors). A similar trend may be observed in all the advanced capitalist countries. In Britain, the number of automobile producers diminished from 88 in 1922 to 20 in 1956, 5 of which accounted for 95 percent of the total production. Among these 5, the biggest and most powerful are international corporations dominated by United States capital—a point to which we shall return in a later context.

The early history of monopoly formation is associated with economic crises and a sharp fall in the rate of profit accompanying them. Generally, alliances and agreements were concluded during and after a crisis as a reaction to declining profit rates. Basing his classification on E. A. G. Robinson (1952:83–95), who distinguished 13 forms of monopoly type agreements, Mandel (1968:401–03) reduced these to 7, which we briefly review here:

1. *Gentlemen's Agreements,* that is, voluntary arrangements among producers "not to sell below certain prices or in certain areas."
2. *Price-regulating associations:* somewhat more formal arrangements and, hence, more effective than gentlemen's agreements.
3. *Pools:* Definite shares of the market are precisely allocated to each producer. "A pool of this kind came into operation fairly soon in the steel-making industry in the United States. The classic example remains the American meatpackers' pool, which carved up the American market for two decades."
4. *Cartels, buying or selling syndicates, sales offices:*

Participating enterprises, while retaining their independence, are nonetheless "bound by more-or-less long-term mutual contracts [and], set up common organizations for buying and selling, and often have to pay heavy fines if they break these agreements."

5. *Trusts:* "Originally, the trust is a grouping to which previously competing companies entrust their shares, receiving in exchange certificates which indicate the proportion in which they participate in the joint effort. Standard Oil was the classical trust in the U.S.A., but it was declared illegal in 1890." "Trust" is now also used as a generic term to refer to any monopoly-type merger.

6. *Holding Company:* This form concentrates the financial control of a number of businesses which retain their formal independence. "The holding company makes it possible to reduce the proportion of capital needed in order to wield effective control over a large number of companies, through various techniques such as 'waterfall'-shareholding or cross-shareholding."

7. *Mergers:* These "are the most 'solid' and lasting form of capitalist concentration, in which all legal or financial independence of the constituent company vanishes. According to their origins, one can distinguish between *horizontal* trusts, formed by the merging of firms in a single branch of industry . . . and *vertical* trusts (grouping firms which reciprocally supply each other's raw materials)."

BANK AND FINANCE CAPITAL

Along with industrial concentration, and often facilitating and controlling it, there proceeded the centralizing of banking and other financial organizations. This process could be observed in *all* capitalist countries until quite recently and it continues to this day. If we center attention on the United States, for example, we find that in 1948, W. W. Aldrich, chairman of the Chase National Bank (Rockefeller group), also was head of: the American Telephone and Telegraph Company, the richest trust; the Metropolitan Insurance Company, the biggest insurance organization; Westinghouse Electric; International Paper; Discount Corporation of New York; and Chase Safe Deposit Company. Thus, one man sat at the apex of an organizational complex controlling "more than 20 billion dollars of capital . . . (the equivalent of three of France's annual budgets at the beginning of the 1950's)" (Mandel, 1968:411–412).

Similarly, in 1948, George Whitney of J. P. Morgan and Company was a director of Consolidated Edison of New York, General Motors Company, Kennecott Copper, the Pullman Company, the Continental Oil Company, and Guaranty Trust.

Finally, R. K. Mellon, chairman of the Mellon National Bank was in the same year "head of the holding companies F. Mellon and Sons and Millbank Corporation and a director of the Aluminum Company of America (Alcoa), the Gulf Oil Company. . . . Westinghouse Air Brake Corporation, the Pittsburgh Plate Glass Company, the Pennsylvania Railroad, . . . Koppers Corporation, the Union Switch and Signal Company," and several large insurance corporations (Mandel, 1968:412).

In addition to the Morgan, Rockefeller, and Mellon groups, there are in the United States at least four more principal financial groups—the Kuhn-Loeb, duPont, Chicago, and Bank of America groups—with a variety of links among all seven. Of course, a similarly small number of powerful groups may be found in every capitalist country.[2]

The predominance of a few large powerful industrial and financial groups makes possible the control of supply and prices, and thereby enables the participants to reap monopoly profits. One striking form of such profits has been called "cartel rent" and may be illustrated by a 1952

---

[2] See Mandel (1968:414–19) for a listing of the interests that each of these groups controls in the major capitalist countries.

report of the United States Department of Commerce. Summarizing some of its findings, Mandel (1968:421) writes that

> the "Big Seven" of the oil industry (Standard Oil of New Jersey, Standard Oil of California, Socony Vacuum Oil, Gulf Oil Corp., Texas Co., Anglo-Iranian—later called British Petroleum—and Royal Dutch Shell) had over a period of years imposed common prices for the oil produced in the Western hemisphere and that produced in the Middle East, though the latter's cost of production was *four to six times lower than that of American Oil*.

Even when explicit agreements do not exist, monopoly prices and profits may be established and sustained through what has been called "price leadership." This takes the form of one unit member of an industry—typically, the biggest and most powerful—leading the way by announcing its prices, with the other units following suit and adopting that price. The variations in price that prevail under these circumstances are confined to very severe limits, a good illustration of which is the present situation in the United States automobile industry.

Whatever the means employed, it is clear that the corporate giants tend to determine prices and take an increasing share of profits. Moreover, profit margins grow with the volume of a company's turnover.

Mandel attributes this to a superiority in productivity and efficiency on the part of the giants. But this proposition should be regarded as problematic. An alternative hypothesis that the greater profit margin is rather a function of economic power should be explored. The connection between profits and economic power is implicit in the organizational methods that the giants employ to enhance their control of supply and price. It is also implicit, for example, in the various "restrictive techniques," enumerated by Mandel, that they employ to adapt production to "effective demand." Because these techniques *restrict* production and are fetters on economic growth, the giants cannot be regarded simultaneously as productive and restrictive. Most important, whether the big corporations are more productive and efficient is still an open question.

Large corporations deliberately restrict production as a matter of policy. This statement is indisputable. In assessing the market, they would prefer to underestimate rather than to overestimate. Overestimating threatens profits and might prove to be disastrous, but underestimating tends to increase profits. This explains why major industries sometimes work at less than full productive capacity—an important point to which we shall return.

For the same general reasons, corporate giants often suppress technical innovations or determine when and how they should be applied according to their interests. Instances of such suppression and delay are numerous and well known. The case of General Electric and Westinghouse is notorious. For ten years, these two firms worked to prevent introduction of fluorescent lighting in this country (Bright, 1949: 308–404). Suppression of the Tucker rear-engine automobile immediately after World War II is another notorious example. This automobile featured an engine that could be removed easily for repairs and for replacement of parts. There are many other examples, which we need not review here. However, Daniel Hamberg (1956:123–24) aptly illustrates the general relation of giant corporations to technical innovation in the following discussion:

> In the modern industrial economy, particularly, the instances are legion in which giant corporations have been major innovators. Careful scrutiny would probably show, however, that in most of these cases the innovations have been noncompetitive with existing products. When they have been competitive, innovations by *existing* firms, as should be expected, have followed long periods of market exploitation of the "old" products. Given this fact (exemplified by the innovational behavior of the electrical manufacturing, radio and television, railway locomotive and telephone industries, among others), we have the pos-

sibility of long lags between the introduction of (competitive) innovations by existing firms who have, for reasons cited above, built up strong monopoly positions. At the same time, the extreme difficulties in assembling the large amounts of capital necessary for modern industrial operations militate strongly against the easy appearance of *new* firms in the role of innovator.

Finally, to the restriction of production and the suppression of innovation, one must add the deteriorating quality of goods resulting from the monopoly power of big firms. By now, this is too well known to require documentation here. With this background in mind, we turn to present-day structures and trends of corporate capitalism. We shall concern ourselves almost exclusively with the United States. However, this focus has nothing to do with ethnocentrism; rather it is dictated by sound theoretical considerations.

5

Corporate Capitalism in the United States

Just as Marx based his model on the most advanced capitalism of his time in England, we must derive our conception of contemporary capitalism from a "study of the United States, which is today as far ahead of other countries in terms of capitalist development as Britain was in the nineteenth century" (Baran and Sweezy, 1966:7).[1]

Earlier, we used the term "giant corporation" several times. This is the concept with which the present discussion begins. Baran and Sweezy present an ideal-type paradigm to bring out clearly the essential characteristics of the U.S. corporation from the standpoint of the structure of power. They begin by emphasizing that management, a board of di-

[1] In the present discussion, I rely mainly on this outstanding work which is to the best of my knowledge the most systematic attempt, from a neo-Marxian standpoint, to advance our *theoretical* grasp of corporate capitalism in the United States.

rectors together with the chief executive officers, controls the corporate organization. Outside interests frequently are represented on the board to harmonize the corporation's interests and policies with those of powerful outsiders such as suppliers, bankers, other corporate customers, and the like. However, insiders, the full-time professional executives whose interests and careers are tied to the corporation's fate, are the ones who actually hold and wield power within it.

A second essential feature is the self-perpetuating character of management, its accountability to the stock-holders being practically nil. Management is self-perpetu-ating in the sense that each generation of managers recruits, trains, and promotes its successors according to its own values and interests. Advance in the corporate career as-sumes two characteristic forms: "rising from lower to higher positions within a given company, and moving from a smaller company to a larger one. The acme of success is the presidency or board chairmanship of one of the biggest corporations" (Baran and Sweezy, 1966:16).

The third important characteristic is the corporation's relative independence from banks and other financial insti-tutions as compared with the early era of monopoly capi-tal. On occasion, the giant corporation may still borrow; but typically, it need not do so because it is capable of generating the capital it requires internally.

Now the point here is not to make light of the impor-tance of great personal and family wealth in gaining for an individual a command post in a corporation. Nevertheless, these assets generally do not enable an individual to control or influence "a giant corporation from the outside. They are rather tickets of admission to the inside, where real corpo-rate power is wielded" (Baran and Sweezy 1966:17). The authors cite C. Wright Mills (1956:116) who made the same point quite effectively:

> Not great fortunes, but great corporations are the important units of wealth, to which individuals of property are variously attached. The corporation

is the source of, and the basis of the continued power and privilege of wealth. All the men and the families of great wealth are now identified with large corporations in which their property is seated.

By stressing that power resides *inside*, not outside, the corporation, Baran and Sweezy are also arguing against the "interest group" conception of present-day capital—a conception that is still prevalent, especially among Marxists. We have seen, for example, that Mandel spoke of the Morgan, Rockefeller, and other interest groups as though they were the prime movers of the economy. Baran and Sweezy (1966:18) deny neither the historical importance nor the considerable influence of such groups today, but they underscore the increasing autonomy of the corporation and the rapidly diminishing importance of interest groups to such a degree, in fact, "that an appropriate model of the economy no longer needs to take account of them."

In an earlier stage of capitalism, industrial corporations were unable to mobilize internally the immense capital outlays they required; these corporations were therefore quite dependent on investment bankers and other financiers. In time, however, huge profits enabled these corporations to generate capital internally and, thus, to gain more and more independence from financial organizations. Correspondingly, corporate policy increasingly was based on the corporation's own interests and not subordinated to the group's.

This tendency is well illustrated by the Rockefeller group, generally acknowledged to be one of the two most powerful. In 1911, the Justice Department invoked terms of the Sherman Act of 1890 to break up Standard Oil Company, a major pillar of the Rockefeller interests, into several separate companies operating in various regions of the country. Nevertheless, until 1929, the companies remained within the interest group that the Rockefeller family continued firmly to control. Each company respected the other's domain and generally cooperated against emerging independents who threatened them from the outside. In

1929, the president of Standard of Indiana attempted to wrest his company's control from the Rockefellers, but he failed and was promptly fired.

After 1929, several important changes occurred in the oil industry, including formation of the international cartel and development of the rich oil fields in the Middle East. Within the United States, the government enforced limitation of oil production to a small fraction of total productive capacity, thereby sustaining monopoly prices effectively throughout the Depression. In the ensuing three decades, the phenomenal growth in the number of automobiles and the increasing substitution of fuel oil for coal produced a rapid and marked rise in both demand and production. The response to these developments provides a sound basis for assessing the validity of the interest-group theory as opposed to the competing hypothesis of corporate autonomy.

> The record leaves little doubt about the answer. California Standard, getting into the Middle-Eastern production in a big way but without adequate marketing outlets, teamed up internationally with Texaco rather than with one of the "brother" companies, and invaded the New England market, traditional stronghold of Jersey and Socony, even at the cost of depressing gasoline prices. The others were not long in following California's example, and by now the various Standard companies have completely broken away from the 1911 marketing areas and are busy stealing markets from each other as well as from the non-Standard companies (Baran and Sweezy, 1966:19).

Information to determine whether the various Standard companies are subject to Rockefeller control in spite of the apparent dissolution is not available. It is possible that the divestiture was a sham. But if this is the case, the Rockefellers must have concluded that it is in their best interests to permit and even encourage each of the separate companies to pursue its interests independently. This would mean that the autonomous corporation is the essential element. It does *not* mean that agreements, groupings, or alignments no longer exist. Indeed, they do exist, but their formation is determined not by powerful outsiders "but by the rational calculation of inside managements. In the oil industry, for example, Standard companies are as ready and willing to ally themselves with or fight against non-Standard companies as with or against other Standard companies. It all depends on where the maximum profit lies" (Baran and Sweezy, 1966:20).

The last sentence of the quote implies that maximization of profit is the major motive of corporate management and, hence, the central mission of the corporate organization. Students of corporations frequently deny this. They describe managers not as planners of strategies that tend to maximize corporate profits, but as neutral technocrats who, in exercising their authority, are highly aware of their responsibility to various publics. According to this view, it is the interests of such publics—stockholders, employees, customers, and others—that management strives to balance in terms of the principles of public policy.

In its extreme form, this view implies that dominance of the great corporations spells the end of capitalism. It also implies that economic rationality or economizing behavior, an essential element of economic theory for centuries, is no longer pertinent to an understanding of the corporation. In its less extreme form, the proponents of this view argue that earning profits that are merely "satisfactory" is the chief motive of management. Surely both of these views are untenable.

Basing their research on an important paper by James S. Earley (1957), Baran and Sweezy (1966) show why this view, although fashionable in some academic and other circles, should not be taken seriously. Earley's research led him to reject the organizational theory developed by Herbert A. Simon and his associates. According to this theory, the typical large-scale U.S. corporation engages in "satisficing" behavior—that is, its management contents itself merely with satisfactory profits. The main evidence against acceptance of this theory may be summarized quite briefly:

1. Management literature unequivocally extols the assessment of management on the basis of the level of cost reduction, expansion of revenue, and increase in profits achieved by the company during a tenure of management;

2. Management of leading, so-called excellently managed companies possessed virtues that enabled their companies to achieve these goals, as shown by Earley's questionnaire studies;

3. The role of economists, market analysts, and other specialists and consultants whose primary mission is to help the firm reduce costs, find superior methods, choose the most profitable alternatives, and uncover new profit opportunities has expanded rapidly in large firms.

In short, the varied and complex application of rational, problem-solving techniques to corporate policy contributes to a profit-oriented rationality that is becoming more, not less, pronounced. Yet Earley's conception does not entirely square with the old postulate of profit maximization, but rather falls somewhere between this postulate and Simon's "satisfactory profit."

Describing his behavioral postulate as "a systematic temporal search for the highest practicable profits," Earley (1957) outlines its accompanying theory: the modern corporation's major goals are "high managerial incomes, good profits, a strong competitive position, and growth." Far from being mutually inconsistent, these goals are complementary. Innovation and substantial expenditure for growth are essential for competitive strength and even for survival. Considering the hazards and frequently the unfeasibility of growth by merger, management's preference for internal financing

> requires high and growing profits above dividend levels. So, too, do high managerial regards. High and rising profits are hence an instrument as well as a direct goal of great importance. With these goals and needs in view, advanced management

plans for profits through time, using coordinated programs stretching as far ahead as practicable. The profit targets incorporated in these programs are sufficient to finance not only good dividends but also desired innovative and growth expenditures (Earley, 1957).

The main tendency, then, is toward profit maximization (highest practicable profit), and because of the rapidly growing application of techniques and expertise, corporate behavior will be "more rather than less appropriately analyzed by some of our time-honored theoretical notions, such as profit maximization" (Earley, 1957).

Earley's most important point is that the modern corporation remains profit-oriented and that the technical and expert knowledge it employs equips it to maximize profits far better than either the classical entrepreneur or earlier corporate firms ever had been. The typical leader who steers the modern corporation toward its goals is neither a tycoon nor an entrepreneur: but rather, he is a professional manager dedicated to advancement of the company—to the expansion of its economic power and profits.

Managers are professionals, but this should not be construed, as it often is, to mean that they are merely a salaried neutral technocracy serving the so-called public interest. Although the issue is still being debated, the findings of C. Wright Mills' (1956) seem closest to the truth: the "corporate rich" and "very rich" are, with few exceptions, overlapping strata. The higher corporate executives are men of wealth and property before they ever join the corporation. And once they take their place in the corporations, they become the most active and influential representatives of great wealth and property.

At least since the early thirties, when Berle and Means (1954) published their now famous *The Modern Corporation and Private Property*, it has been fashionable to speak of the "separation of ownership from control." Some observers construe this phrase to imply that there is no longer any connection between the ownership and control of wealth and property. There is a grain of truth here: management is no longer subject to the control of its shareholders—especially the multitude of small ones. Nevertheless, managers are not in a separate class. They are owners of large holdings, they occupy strategic positions, and, as such, they comprise a leading stratum of the rich and propertied class.

As we have said, the executive is devoted to advancing the economic power of his firm—and thereby himself, we should add. His standing among managers in general is measured by his company's financial assets and sphere of influence and by the level of his position in the company. His organization, not so much his personal qualities, endows him with respect and "greatness." Insofar as he advances his company organization, he advances himself. But how is a company's advancement assessed?

Size is one important index; strength, "measured by such standards as credit rating and the price of a company's securities, is another" (Baran and Sweezy, 1966:39). The rate of growth is also a valuable measure. Other things being equal, the more rapidly growing firm also will have the higher standing. Ultimately, however, these indices depend on profit; a firm that fails to maximize its profits cannot increase its strength and ensure its growth.

Having achieved success, the modern corporation flaunts its status in the form of imposing structures, plush executive suites, company-owned fleets of jet planes, and the like. At the same time, the successful corporation can indulge in philanthropy—supporting universities, research projects, and foundations—but with one eye on the benefits it might reap from tax savings and basic scientific research and the other on improving its public image.

In short, the giant corporation is contemporary capitalism's main agency for the maximization of profits and accumulation of capital. The antitrust movement never succeeded in restoring competition, but it did place "very real roadblocks in the way of full monopolization" (Baran and Sweezy, 1966:51). The mode of interaction among the corporate giants, is neither full monopoly nor unbridled competition; nonetheless, it carries with it some of the classical contradictions of capitalism.

RISING SURPLUS: A TENDENTIAL LAW
OF CORPORATE CAPITALISM

Under competitive capitalism, the enterprise is a "price-taker"; under corporate capitalism, the giant corporation is a "price-maker" (Scitovsky, 1951:18, 20). Since neither perfect competition nor full monopoly prevails, price-making assumes a specific form. The corporate giant cannot vary its prices at will. Indeed, even if it were a monopolist, it could not do so. As the sole seller of a given commodity for which no substitutes exist, a perfect monopolist can lower his prices, and as the price drops, people will buy more of his goods. Because there are no rivals with a similar product, there is no one to retaliate. According to monopoly price theory, the monopolist's problem under these hypothetical conditions is relatively simple. He lowers his price until the additional revenue from the sale of an extra unit—bearing in mind that the price of all preceding units also declines—is precisely equal to the additional costs incurred in producing the extra unit. "Up to this point, producing and selling an additional unit brings in more revenue than it adds to costs; beyond this point, the reverse is true. Hence this point defines the price and output which maximize the monopolists' profit" (Baran and Sweezy, 1966:57). Because corporate giants are not perfect monopolists, their approach to determining prices is not so simple. Clearly, if one giant should decide to lower prices in order to increase demand and thereby his profits, the effect would be felt by the others producing the same commodity. Quite soon, no doubt, the other firms would react and try to win back the customers they had lost by lowering their own prices, perhaps even underselling the original price-cutter. What therefore began as an effort to improve the position of one, probably would end in a worse position for all.

Assuming that such competitive conditions exist among several giants, even the fullest information about demand for the total industry's products and its own costs will not enable a single corporation to know what price is likely to maximize its profits. This is so because the market of a single corporation is determined not only by its own price, but its rivals' prices as well. Obviously, this information cannot be known in advance. Consequently, the most careful estimate of the profit-maximizing price is a mere guess because never can a corporation be absolutely certain of its rivals' reactions. A wrong guess could provoke a series of moves and countermoves culminating in mutually disastrous price warfare.

This type of situation was quite common in the early days of monopoly capitalism and may be observed occasionally in certain industries even today, but it is no longer typical. Today, corporations strive to minimize risk and uncertainty by effectively banning price competition as an economic weapon. Corporation leaders have learned from experience that this policy best serves their mutual interests.

What, then, is the guiding principle under oligopolistic conditions? Several large vendors have an interest in establishing prices in a way that will maximize profits. None has an interest in reducing the total volume of profits and together they constitute a monopoly or quasi-monopoly. The situation is not much different from the one for which monopoly price theory was developed. The ideal exceptional case of classical and neo-classical economics has become the actual general case. Price theory under oligopoly is not fundamentlly different from what it would be under monopoly.

How are the prices actually arrived at in an oligopolistic situation? At one time, *open* collusion was the rule in the United States. The antitrust laws effectively brought this to an end.[2] Today, the typical process appears to be a form of implicit coordination that has come to be called "price leadership." Price leadership prevails when one firm announces the price at which it plans to sell a product or service and the others follow suit. Generally, the price leader is the largest and most powerful member of an industry—for example, General Motors and U.S. Steel. Their leadership is accepted by the smaller and less powerful firms because the

[2] No doubt secret collusion continues. For a well documented case involving the electrical giants, see *Fortune Magazine* (1961).

smaller firms know that they are the ones most likely to lose by price warfare.

In some industries and situations, however, regular patterns of price leadership are not readily discernible: taking the initiative appears to be an arbitrary matter. Furthermore, the initial announcement of a price change may only be a trial balloon. If the others follow suit, the price change remains in effect; if not, it is rescinded. In this way, the firms communicate their intentions and work their way to a price that in any given period is "a reasonable approximation to the theoretical monopoly price" (Baran and Sweezy, 1966:62).

Nonetheless, the difference between price changes under "perfect" monopoly and oligopoly is significant. In response to changing conditions, monopoly prices may be raised or lowered—the sole consideration being which course of action is likely to better one's profit position. Under oligopoly, in contrast, the implications of raising and lowering prices differ. If one seller raises his prices, the others cannot construe his move as a hostile act. At worst, the others will refrain from following suit so that he is forced either to rescind his offer or content himself with a smaller slice of the market. On the other hand, if a seller assumes the initiative and lowers his prices, the others could interpret this move as hostile because the initiator appears to be trying to enlarge his portion of the market by breaking the ban on price competition. Should his rivals thus construe his act, the result could be a price war injurious to all. Therefore,

> everyone concerned is likely to be more circumspect about lowering prices than raising prices. Under oligopoly, in other words, prices tend to be stickier on the downward side than on the upward side, and *this fact introduces a significant upward bias into the general price level in a monopoly capitalist enconomy* (Baran and Sweezy, 1966: 63–64; italics added).

We are now approaching the main subject of this section—the tendency of the surplus to rise. Baran and Sweezy

(1966:9) have defined economic surplus as "the difference between what a society produces and the costs of producing it." Banning price competition in an oligopoly does not mean that all forms of competition have ceased. For now, we will limit our attention to one form that relates to costs of production and, therefore, to the size of the economic surplus. The major thesis is simple:

> If oligopolies succeed in attaining a close approximation to the theoretical monopoly price and if their never-ceasing efforts to cut costs . . . are generally successful, then it follows with inescapable logic that surplus must have a strong and persistent tendency to rise (Baran and Sweezy, 1966:67).

To understand and accept this conclusion, one must understand why the corporate giants continually strive to lower their costs.

Firms that keep their costs at a low level have a variety of advantages over their rivals whose costs are higher. The firm with the lowest costs can threaten and even precipitate a price war; it can employ tactics and gain credit and discount favors that the weaker firms cannot use or obtain without provoking damaging retaliation. Low-cost, high-profit firms can best afford advertising, research, new product varieties, the provision of extra services and the like. Clearly, these advantages enable the low-cost firm to capture a larger share of the market. In addition, the reputation of being a low-cost firm attracts new customers and gifted executives and graduates of business and engineering schools. Thus, there are many reasons why each giant strives incessantly to reduce its costs lower and more rapidly than the costs of its competitors.

Those who fall behind in the cost-cutting race become progressively weaker, until they are confronted with the alternatives of merging with a stronger company at disadvantageous terms, staging a comeback with new management and new capital, or leaving the field to its stronger competitors.

Another important source of the tendency for production costs to decline under oligopoly often is neglected. This source is found in the *producers' goods* industries. Here, as in the consumers' goods industries, refraining from price competition is the rule, and sellers continually seek to enlarge their share of the market by producing new products. Because the customers of manufacturers of producers' goods are themselves producers whose main concern is to increase profits, the new product must be designed to generate greater profits by reducing costs of production.

Throughout the business world, the producers of products used in manufacturing machines, computers, automatic equipment, new materials, alloys, plastics, fabrics, and chemicals, for example provide their customers with means of producing at lower costs. Baran and Sweezy (1966:71) therefore conclude that

> with regard to the cost discipline which it imposes on its members the monopoly capitalist economy is no less severe than its competitive predecessor, and that in addition it generates new and powerful impulses to innovation. There can therefore be no doubt about the downward trend of production costs under monopoly capitalism.

It goes without saying that because the object of lowering costs is to expand profits, the rising productivity is not used for the benefit of the great majority of the people. The profit motive remains in effect, as do its consequences: where there is no effective demand, there might just as well be no human needs or wants. The corporations reap the rich fruits of higher productivity and declining production costs in higher profits. Under oligopoly, incessant cost reduction implies expanding profit margins; in turn, expanding profit margins mean

> aggregate profits which rise not only absolutely but as a share of the national product. If we provisionally equate aggregate profits with society's economic surplus, we can formulate as a law of monopoly capitalism that the surplus tends to rise

both absolutely and relatively as the system develops (Baran and Sweezey, 1966:72).[3]

If this analysis is correct, Marx's tendential law of the falling rate of profit, which was based on competitive capitalism, must be replaced by a new law characteristic of oligopolistic capitalism. In the words of Baran and Sweezy (1966:72),

> by substituting the law of rising surplus for the law of falling profit, we are therefore not rejecting or revising a time-honored theorem of political economy: we are simply taking account of the undoubted fact that the structure of the capitalist economy has undergone a fundamental change since that theorem was formulated. What is most essential about the structural change from competitive to monopoly capitalism finds its theoretical expression in this substitution.

If the tendential law of rising surplus is indeed presently operative, the surplus must somehow be absorbed or an economic crisis will arise. How does contemporary corporate capitalism in the United States cope with this problem?

ABSORBING THE SURPLUS

Baran and Sweezy (1966) demonstrate quite effectively that capitalists' consumption and investment are not sufficient to absorb the surplus and thus maintain the system in operation. The tendential law of the rising surplus, as the authors have expounded it, assumes that the economy is operating at

[3] The authors understand quite well that "statistically recorded profits are far from comprising the entire economic surplus. Interest and rent are also forms of surplus; and . . . under monopoly capitalism still other forms assume decisive importance [Nevertheless, they regard] the difference between sales revenue and costs of production . . . a legitimate first approximation to a fully developed concept of the economic surplus" (Baran and Sweezy, 1966:72, footnote 22).

full capacity. The law has its source not in varying operating rates (the ratio of actual production to capacity), but in oligopolistic price and cost policies. But assuming that production is at less than capacity, this has definite implications for the size of the surplus.

As production declines below capacity, the surplus also decreases rapidly, while the investment-seeking part of the surplus contracts even more rapidly. Conversely, as the economy approaches its full operating rate, both the surplus and its investment-seeking portion grow in absolute as well as in relative terms. The relationships have been well established through a careful study of the profitability schedules of major large corporations over a number of decades.

As the recent history of the United States economy in so-called peacetime has shown, both contraction of the economy and its relative expansion fail to achieve either full utilization of productive capacity or full employment. This means that processes internal to the system tend to generate a growing portion of investment-seeking surplus without generating corresponding investment outlets. If corporate capitalism had to rely only on such endogenous investment outlets, chronic depression would result.

But there are also exogenous investments. Economists have drawn attention to three major types: (1) investment to accommodate a growing population; (2) investment in novel production methods and products; and (3) investment abroad. Baran and Sweezy argue convincingly that taken alone or together, none of these types is likely to absorb the rising surplus.

With regard to the first type of investment, the authors reaffirm the position of classical economics: population expansion is more a dependent than an independent variable. Perhaps the growth of population does bring into being some investment outlets, but much importance should not be attributed to this factor. The reasons for this become evident if we bear in mind that purchasing power, not population growth itself, counts.

New methods and products are not likely to constitute

an important outlet. What Baran and Sweezy (1966) have in mind here is the normal process of technical innovation. They readily acknowledge the market-creating effects of what they call "epoch-making" inventions (such as the steam engine, the railroad, and the automobile) and they devote a truly fascinating chapter to the historical impact of these inventions. But these were unique events that happened infrequently. Obviously, one cannot count on such epoch-making, market-creating breakthroughs. Under oligopoly, there is absolutely no necessary relationship between technical advances and the opening of investment outlets. "Technological progress tends to determine the *form* which investment takes at any given time rather than its amounts" (Baran and Sweezy, 1966:97).

Indeed, considering the enormous depreciation allowances of present-day, corporate capitalism, "it is quite possible that business can finance from this source alone all the investment it considers profitable to make in innovations (both new products and new processes), leaving no 'innovational' outlets to help absorb investment-seeking surplus" (Baran and Sweezy, 1966:102). Support for this proposition is provided by the relation of expenditures for research and development, plant and equipment, and depreciation allowances. While expenditures for research and development continued to rise from 1957 to 1962, "outlays on plant and equipment fluctuated around an average of some 8 percent below the 1957 level" (Baran and Sweezy, 1966:103). At the same time, depreciation allowances continued to rise, "with a resultant increase in the proportion of plant and equipment outlays covered by depreciation from under 50 percent in 1953 to over 80 percent in 1962" (Baran and Sweezy, 1966:103).

It is interesting that as I write, President Nixon is promising the corporations even greater depreciation allowances than they now have. Here is Senator Eagleton's (D-Mo.) reaction (March 19, 1971):

On January 11, President Nixon announced new depreciation rules allowing businesses a

faster writeoff of expenditures for new equipment. The change will result in a reduction of
Federal revenues of $2.7 billion in FY 1972, rising
to $4.1 billion in FY 1976. This is roughly equiva-
lent to a 7-percent tax cut for corporate business.
Capital spending experienced a boom throughout
the 1960s, increasing considerably faster than
output. As a result of that boom, and of the recent
down-turn, business is now operating at 76 percent of capacity. It is, therefore, hard to believe
that firms have much of an incentive to increase
investment in equipment. The new rules represent
a windfall gain for business. Businessmen cannot
buy machines for the sake of buying machines;
they do so with the expectation that they will be
able to produce and sell goods at a profit. This expectation of production at a profit will continue to
be absent until something is done to stimulate
consumer demand. What is hard is understanding
how the President can allocate $2.7 billion to cor-
porate profits while vetoing funds for job training
and public service jobs.

In a nutshell, this is why technical innovation is not likely
to contribute to absorption of the surplus, nor is foreign
investment likely to do so. This is so primarily because no
matter how much capital flows out of the United States each
year, returns are consistently much bigger. From 1950 to
1963, for instance, U.S. corporations took in as income "$12
billion more than they sent out as capital, while at the same
time expanding their foreign holdings (through reinvesting
profits earned abroad, borrowing from foreign banks and
investors, etc.) by $28.8 billion" (Baran and Sweezy, 1966:
107). Foreign investment, therefore, appears to aggravate
rather than to alleviate the surplus-absorption problem.

The foregoing discussion thus points to a powerful
tendency which, if unchecked, would necessarily culminate
in permanent economic depression. Clearly, this has not
happened; obviously, countervaling forces are at work. It
is to these forces, which Baran and Sweezy call the "sales
effort," "civilian government," and "militarism and imperialism," that we now briefly turn.

THE SALES EFFORT

The sales effort assumes a qualitatively new role under corporate capitalism. Included in this effort are advertising, modifying the appearance and packaging of commodities, built-in obsolescence, a complex variety of credit schemes, and so forth. This effort has expanded as price competition has declined. In fact, sales effort has supplanted price competition as a means of attracting the potential customer's attention and winning him over. Advertising, the heart of the effort, has become a major form of corporate competition.

Under oligopoly, each of a relatively small number of giant firms accounts for a large proportion of the total output of a single product. Prices among the firms vary insignificantly or not at all. As a result, sellers have resorted to advertising, packaging, and other devices to persuade consumers that each trademark and brand name represents a genuinely different product, not merely an insignificant variation of the same generic item.

Moreover, although this method of persuasion now is applied primarily to consumers' goods, it is being used increasingly in the field of producer goods as well. "It is enough to look at any of the innumerable general and specialized magazines addressed to businessmen," Baran and Sweezy correctly observe, "to become convinced that even highly informed, technically competent buyers are by no means impervious to the appeal of advertising" (Baran and Sweezy, 1968:117).

Advertising creates new but artificial wants. It is manipulative. The greater these wants, the greater the prices giant firms can charge and, therefore, the greater their profits. Historically, continuously rising advertising expenditures signify widening profit margins and declining price competition. In 1890, advertising expenditures amounted to $360 million, in 1929, they totaled $3,426 million, 10 times more than the total expenditures in 1867 (U.S. Bureau of the Census, 1960:526). By 1962, these expenditures had mounted to $12 billion and, since then, probably have doubled.

The rapid rise in allocation of resources to advertising has accompanied the development of corporate capitalism. Accordingly, advertising has changed. Far from being a mere spur to selling, as it was in the competitive era, advertising now is an essential element in the profit-maximizing policy of the corporation.

Essentially, the role of advertising has not been well understood. Many critics have berated it for increasing the advertiser's income at the expense of consumers, for inducing consumers to base their decisions on irrational grounds, for squandering resources, and for many other evils. But few observers are aware of its most significant consequence: it expands phenomenally the total volume of consumption and therefore increasingly serves corporate capital as a necessary and indispensable means of absorbing part of the economic surplus (Baran and Sweezy, 1966:124).

Like government spending, sales effort expands income and output, but the sales effort also creates new capital investment opportunities by expanding demand for products. Whether it actually is a new product or merely a new brand does not matter in this context. To be sure, the latter case involves a waste of resources. Nevertheless, these resources would not have been utilized in the present economy normally operating at less than full capacity and employment. For this reason, advertising makes for a net increment to investment and income.

Furthermore, advertising and sales effort generally invade the production process itself. The most well-known forms of invasion range from the simple, inexpensive packaging gimmicks employed by many industries to the complex, expensive model changes made in the automobile industry annually. Today, more than ever before, the sales department determines what will be produced and how it will be produced. In much the same way, the object of multibillion dollar research and development programs funded by large U.S. corporations is to produce saleable goods, not to advance science and technology. By now, it is common knowledge that such practices result in production of inferior products. The fact that a major form of this quality deterioration is planned obsolescence is also well known; nevertheless, many consumers are unaware that built-in obsolescence constitutes a masked price increase because the products for which they pay have a short life-expectancy and, frequently, will require ongoing, expensive repair bills.

And yet, if maintaining the economy is the criterion, built-in obsolescence and frequent style changes (which often amount to the same thing) have their positive effects —namely, "a stepping up in the rate of replacement demand and a general boost to income and employment. In this respect as in others, the sales effort turns out to be a powerful antidote to monopoly capitalism's tendency to sink into a state of chronic depression" (Baran and Sweezy, 1966:131). In these terms, the sales effort contributes to maintaining the economy in motion under conditions best suited to the corporations' central and most abiding interest—profit maximization.

CIVILIAN GOVERNMENT

Classical and neo-classical economics as well as Marxian political economics generally assumed that the industrial plant operated at full capacity. From this, it followed that the expenses of government had to be taken from the total social output. In addition, they assumed that the workers' wages or conventional subsistence were held at a minimal level by powerful economic and social forces such as the "industrial reserve army." The conclusion followed naturally that the financial burden of government would fall on those classes that receive portions of the economic surplus in the form of profit, rent, or interest, and that the income these classes otherwise would have consumed or invested would instead be taxed to cover the expense of state. Little wonder, then, in light of this economic theory, that the wealthy and privileged supported the principle that the best government is that which governs least.

Under corporate capitalism, the situation is quite different. Normally, as we have seen, the productive plant operates at less than full capacity. The economic system fails to generate sufficient effective demand to achieve and maintain full capacity and employment. If these unused "resources can be put to work, they can produce not only necessary means of subsistence for the producers, but also additional amounts of surplus. Hence, if government creates more effective demand, it can increase its command over goods and services without encroaching on the incomes of its citizens (Baran and Sweezy, 1966:143). Government can create effective demand through direct purchases of goods and services or by means of transfer payments such as subsidies to business and agriculture, compensation to the unemployed, pensions to the retired and aged, and so forth.

Keynes and his followers first pointed out these possibilities in a systematic way. For a while, however, it was believed that effective demand could be created only if the government's spending exceeded its income, making up the difference through deficit financing—borrowing, printing additional money, and the like. Economists now generally reject this view. Instead, they believe that in an economy working at less than total capacity, government can generate additional demand even when the budget is balanced. In the United States, total government spending has served to create demand and therefore to absorb part of the surplus.

The increased importance of government's role in spending may be illustrated as follows: expressed as a percentage of GNP, government spending climbed from 9.8 in 1929 to 28.8 in 1961 (Baran and Sweezy, 1966:146). The important and increasingly active role of government spending as a means of creating demand and absorbing surplus is typical of all advanced capitalist countries and, indeed, of all expanding economies, capitalist or not.

In the United States, increasing government expenditures for civilian purposes definitely have *not* been made at the expense of corporations. The expenditures have not been deductions from what corporations and individuals otherwise would have spent for their own private demands. In the absence of government spending, the rising surplus characteristic of corporate capitalism never would have been absorbed through private channels. Consequently, assuming that there are no other outlets, it would not have been produced at all. "What government absorbs," Baran and Sweezy (1966:147) emphasize, "is in addition to, not subtracted from, private surplus." Apart from the. Depression years, the rise in corporate taxation has not reduced corporate profits after taxes.

Generally, representatives of big business understand that taxes do not constitute a deduction from their private surplus. They understand too that government spending means effective demand and that their taxes can be shifted onto the shoulders of consumers or workers or both. Economists also generally understand this.

Now, consider the facts: under corporate capitalism, private interests cannot themselves absorb the surplus; government spending activates otherwise idle resources and creates income and jobs; and, finally, the cost is not borne by the corporations. Under these conditions, it is not surprising that neither labor nor management now oppose government spending. To put it positively, both support it.

What must be stressed here is that in spite of the vast and growing increase in government spending as a percentage of GNP in the years since 1929, "almost nine-tenths [of the increase comprised] transfer payments and defense purchases, little more than one-tenth non-defense purchases" (Baran and Sweezy, 1966:152). While transfer payments (allocations for Social Security, unemployment, and old-age, and veterans benefits, for example) have increased as a percentage of GNP (from 1.6 percent in 1929 to 5.9 percent in 1957), other allocations for the welfare of the citizen have grown "only about as fast as the economy as a a whole" (Baran and Sweezy, 1966:153). No matter what the spending is for—public housing, education, public health and medicine, or another essential human need—some powerful vested interest will oppose increased government spending for that purpose.

On the other hand, military spending, as everyone knows, has risen astronomically since the Second World War. In the mid-1960s, more than 9 percent of the labor force depended on the military budget for employment. Indeed, military spending has been the key factor in maintaining employment and using and absorbing surplus capacity. In 1939, unemployment stood at 17.2 percent of the labor force and about 1.4 percent was involved in production for the military. In 1961, the figures were 6.7 percent and 9.4 percent, respectively. Clearly,

> the percentage of the labor force either unemployed or dependent on military spending was much the same in 1961 as in 1939. From which it follows that if the military budget were reduced to 1939 proportions, unemployment would also revert to 1939 proportions (Baran and Sweezy, 1966:176).

Familiarity with the causes and consequences of the emergence and massive expansion of the military-industrial complex since World War II is essential to an understanding of the economic and social system in the United States today. These causes and consequences are bound up with the developing international role of the United States since that war. Therefore, we must explore the nature of the relations between the United States and other countries. Most important, we must determine whether, on the basis of objective criteria, the relationship of the United States to other nations may be described as a form of imperial domination. An adequate approach to this question requires some background knowledge of the history and theory of imperialism.

6

Imperialism: J. A. Hobson's Pioneering Study

Most, if not all, of the essential characteristics of modern imperialism were admirably described by the well-known British scholar, J. A. Hobson (1971),[1] a liberal in the classical sense and a non-Marxist. Hobson developed his conception independent of his Marxist contemporary, Rudolf Hilferding,[2] but he exercised a profound influence on Hilferding as well as on such other famous Marxists as Karl Kautsky, Rosa Luxembourg, and, of course, Vladimer I. Lenin. Indeed, his influence on Lenin was so great that one might justifiably refer to his elaboration as the Hobson-Lenin theory of imperialism.

The fundamental difference between the two was that

[1] Originally published in 1902.

[2] Most probably, Hobson was also unaware of the scattered suggestive comments about the emerging imperialism that Marx and Engels had made in *Capital* (1962) and other writings.

Hobson regarded the developing imperialism as a powerful but not unavoidable policy under capitalism, while Lenin viewed imperialism as an inevitable stage in capitalism's development. Lenin accepted Hobson's description of what was in fact happening, but rejected what he called Hobson's pacifist, reformist conclusions. By thus accepting much of Hobson's analysis and rejecting his conclusions, Lenin sought to build the analysis of imperialism into Marxist theory. Just how great was the extent of Lenin's intellectual indebtedness to Hobson, may be seen from a brief resume of Hobson's remarkable study.

The new and dangerous aspect of the developing imperialism was its nationalistic aggressiveness. It crushed the spirit of internationalism by transforming the nations of Europe into rival empires, engaged in a cutthroat struggle. At the same time, European domination of the weaker, non-European nations stimulated among the latter a national self-consciousness that bristled with resentment toward their oppressors. The new imperialism consisted of several chauvinistic and antagonistic nation-states, each bent on territorial, commercial, and industrial aggrandizement—at both the expense of one another and the weaker colonial peoples. This development was "not intelligible without a close analysis of those conditions of modern capitalist production which compel an ever keener 'fight for markets'" (Hobson, 1971:12).

The political manifestations of the new antagonisms of interest were obvious. Every nation on the European continent was pouring an ever-increasing share of its resources into military armaments and naval equipment; peace appeared to be perpetually menaced; and new powers, such as the United States, were entering the competition. Accompanying these developments were new jingoistic doctrines for popular consumption, a new cynical and calculating *real-Politik,* and sliding scale of diplomatic language such as "hinterland, sphere of interest, sphere of influence, paramountcy, suzerainty, [and] protectorate," (Hobson, 1971:13).

For Hobson, as for Lenin and other Marxists, the new imperialism dated from 1870, gaining momentum in the

1880s. Beginning in 1884, the vast territories of Africa were partitioned, adding some three and three-quarter millions of square miles to the British Empire within fifteen years. But Britain was not alone in this new expansionism. In the same period, Germany began its expansionist policy in Africa and in the Oceanic islands, bringing under her sway some one million square miles and fourteen million people. France, too, extended her empire in Senegal, the Sahara, and Tunisia in the 1880s and at the same time consolidated her hold on parts of Indo-China. In somewhat the same way, Italy and Belgium and, to a lesser extent, Portugal entered the scramble for Africa. Russia and the United States entered the competition each in its own way. Russia annexed portions of Asia and the United States established protectorates in the Pacific islands and took over the remains of the old Spanish empire. Hobson perceived that the most advanced and rapidly developing capitalist countries were the primary participants in the new imperialism; the older and capitalistically less advanced colonial powers such as Spain and Holland played a diminishing role in the new expansion.

Directing his fire mainly against British imperialists, Hobson (1971:23) showed that not a single one of the 39 areas that Great Britain annexed after 1870 was "endowed with responsible self-government." With the exception of the South African states, settled by significant numbers of white men, the new colonies, thickly peopled by "lower races" were deprived of self-rule. Because the imposition of autocratic rule was equally characteristic of the other European colonizers, politically, "the new imperialism was an expansion of autocracy" (Hobson, 1971:27).

Hobson's main purpose in this study was to demonstrate that the new imperialism had an insignificant commercial value and that therefore it was an irrational and unnecessary policy. He demonstrated with abundant data that Britain's imperialist expansion had not been accompanied by an increase in the value of her trade with her colonies and dependencies. Nevertheless, during the same period, the value of British trade with independent foreign nations had increased substantially. In fact, the greatest increase in trade had been with precisely those nations that Britain regarded as her major industrial and colonial rivals—Germany, France, Russia, and the United States.

The conclusion was inescapable: commercially, the tropical and subtropical regions added by British imperialism were those with which trade was "small, precarious, and unprogressive." Only with the "genuine colonies" of Australia, Canada, and Cape Colony had the volume of trade increased. As for trade with the other newly added territories, it formed "an utterly insignificant part of our national income, while the expenses connected directly and indirectly with the acquisition, administration and defense of these possessions must swallow an immeasurably larger sum" (Hobson, 1971:39).

In addition, the newly acquired possessions provided no outlets for the so-called surplus population. Here, again, Hobson wanted effectively to refute the prevalent view to the contrary and demonstrate that imperialism was unnecessary. The new territories furnished employment to a very thin stratum of the upper classes: a few prospectors, missionaries, engineers, overseers, and the like, and that is all.

Obviously, the new imperialism was an unwise policy from a number of standpoints. From the standpoint of the British economy as a whole any gains resulting from imperialistic policy were small, poor, and precarious, and far outweighed by the enormous expenditures entailed in procuring and protecting them. At the same time, the policy roused both the resentment of oppressed peoples and the hostility of rival nations. This lead Hobson (1971:46) to the central question of his study: "How is the British nation induced to embark upon such unsound business? The only possible answer," he replies, "is that the business interests of the nation as a whole are subordinated to those of certain sectional interests that usurp control of the national resources and use them for their private gain." [3]

---

[3] Hobson's logic is therefore quite different from the line of reasoning that rejects the hypothesis that the United States is an imperialistic power simply on the ground that exports and foreign investment are minor elements in the total U.S. economy. This argument is encountered occasionally even today.

Unquestionably, imperialism has been bad for the national economy as a whole. This does not mean that no one
gained from the policy. There is no doubt that certain classes
reaped great benefits, not only from the vast human and
material resources spent on armaments and wars, but from
the checks effectively placed on political and social reforms
as well. Therefore, the present policy must not be attributed
to the victory of some ultimate irrationalism in politics.

No! Neither blind national passions nor the folly of
ambitious politicians accounts for imperialism. An analysis
of the connection between politics and business will show
imperialist policy to be far more rational than it appears at
first sight: "Irrational from the standpoint of the whole
nation, it is rational enough from the standpoint of certain
classes in the nation" (Hobson, 1971:47). Neither a rational, well-planned socialism nor an intelligent *laissez-faire*
capitalism would tolerate imperialism. Each would rid itself
of the policy. But

> a State in which certain well-organized business
> interests are able to outweigh the weak, diffused
> interest of the community is bound to pursue a
> policy which accord with the pressure of the
> former interests (Hobson, 1971:47–48).

Hobson proceeded to substantiate his hypothesis with respect to Britain by showing, first, that such well-organized
interests did in fact exist and, second, that they effectively
worked their will in the arena of politics.

Who were some of these organized interests? Millions
of pounds of public funds expended for armaments and
other military purposes flowed directly into the tills of certain big industrial firms and indirectly into the various
subsidiaries serving them. In addition, giant manufacturers
for export trade pushed "textiles and hardware, engines,
tools, machinery, spirits, [and] guns, upon new markets.
. . . The making of railways, canals, and other public
works, the establishment of factories, the development of
mines, the improvement of agriculture in new countries,
stimulate a definite interest in important manufacturing
industries which feeds a very firm imperialist faith in their

owners" (Hobson, 1971:49). There were, then, a variety of manufacturing and other economic groups with a direct or indirect interest in the new policy. But numerous individuals in the military, political, diplomatic, clerical, professional, academic, and other circles also acquired a strong interest in imperialism.

Most important was foreign investment. All advanced capitalist nations invested an increasing share in foreign and colonial areas and derived growing income from them. Data revealed that profit from foreign investment far exceeded that of ordinary import-export trade. Hobson (1971: 53–54) writes that

> it is not too much to say, that the modern foreign policy of Great Britain has been primarily a struggle for profitable markets of investment. To a larger extent every year Great Britain has been becoming a nation living upon tribute from abroad, and the classes who enjoy this tribute have had an ever-increasing incentive to employ the public policy, the public purse, and the public force to extend the field of their private investments, and to safeguard and improve their existing investments.

This applied *mutatis mutandis* to Germany, France, and the United States.

Like Hilferding (1968), Hobson also stressed the role of financiers and bankers, "the central ganglion of international capitalism. These powerful interests thrive most directly on the creation of a large public debt. In the United States, for example, the "public financial arrangements for the Philippine war put several millions of dollars into the pockets of Mr. Pierpont Morgan and his friends" (Hobson, 1971:57). In general, these financial giants profited most from the opening up of new territories and the enormous expenditures for military operations and became the guiding and directing force of the new imperialism.

Thus, Hobson argued that Britain's recent expansion and annexations had yielded poor returns for the nation as a whole. Her trade with the other industrially advanced countries had been much more profitable than her trade with the colonial possessions had been. Nonetheless, imperialist policy prevailed because the vested interests who profited most from militarism and expansionism were powerful enough to induce the government to persist in the policy.

THE ECONOMIC TAPROOT OF IMPERIALISM

The pro-imperialist argument held that the great and growing productive capacity of modern industrial capitalism made imperialist expansion absolutely unavoidable. Territorial expansion provided sources of food and raw materials for the burgeoning urban-industrial populations; markets for a growing volume of manufactured goods; and investment outlets for surplus capital, all of which were necessary and unavailable from any other source.

Hobson did not deny that these were powerful economic factors militating toward an imperialist politics at home and abroad. Indeed, he believed that the force of the pro-imperialist argument could be seen in the recent history of the United States. The beginning of its imperial career could be traced directly to economic sources. Aided by its immense natural and human resources and the protection afforded by a high tariff wall, the United States economy had experienced an exceptionally rapid industrialization and became one of the most advanced industrial nations of the world in the span of a single generation. This process was marked by the decline of cutthroat competition, the acceleration of capital concentration, and the increasing amalgamation of industries into trusts. Outlets for profitable investments within the country's own boundaries failed to keep pace with savings. The productive forces far outstripped the rate of consumption, and outside markets appeared to be the sole solution. In Hobson's (1971:77–79) words:

> It was this sudden demand for foreign markets for manufactures and for investments which

was avowedly responsible for the adoption of Imperialism as a political policy and practice by the
Republican party to' which the great industrial
and financial chiefs belonged and which belonged
to them. . . . It was Messrs. Rockefeller, Pierpont Morgan, and his associates who needed Imperialism and who fastened it upon the shoulders
of the great Republic of the West. They needed
Imperialism because they desired to use the public
resources of their country to find profitable employment for their capital which otherwise would
be superfluous. . . .

American Imperialism was the natural product
of the economic pressure of a sudden advance of
capitalism which could not find occupation at home
and needed foreign markets for goods and for investments.

The United States was not alone. All advanced capitalist countries were embarrassed by surplus-capital and "overproduction" as the periodic depressions clearly indicated.
Accordingly, financiers, industrialists, and merchants put
more and more pressure on their governments to acquire
some undeveloped area. Some features were common to all
capitalist countries: an excess of capital seeking profitable
investment; overproduction; centralization of the economy
in trusts and other monopoly forms; and, finally, an aggressive foreign policy bent on acquiring new undeveloped territories. Because these features were common to all, imperialism appeared to be a necessary and inevitable concomitant
of a certain stage of capitalism. Later, Lenin did in fact conclude that modern imperialism is the highest or monopoly
stage of capitalism. Not so Hobson.

Hobson readily acknowledged that the conditions of
contemporary capitalism—mainly, so-called excess productive capacity and surplus investment-seeking capital—
constitute the "taproot of Imperialism," but he denied that
these conditions were unavoidable; from this conclusion, it
followed that imperialism was an excrescence on an otherwise healthy body. Imperialism was a pathological but cura-
ble form of capitalism, not its highest and inevitable stage:

> If the consuming public in this country raised its
> standard of consumption to keep pace with every
> rise of productive powers, there could be no excess
> of goods or capital clamorous to use Imperialism
> in order to find markets: foreign trade would in-
> deed exist, but there would be no difficulty in ex-
> changing a small surplus of our manufactures for
> the food and raw material we annually absorbed,
> and all the savings that we made could find em-
> ployment, if we chose, in home industries (Hob-
> son, 1971:81).

"Why should there be oversaving and overproduction?"
Hobson asked. Why should wants not keep up with the
capacity to satisfy them? If different economic principles
were operative, principles according to which the fulfillment
of human needs was paramount, then "consumption would
rise with every rise of producing power, for human needs
are illimitable, and there could be no excess of saving"
(Hobson, 1971:83). The prevailing economic system does
quite the reverse. It assigns "to some people a consuming
power vastly in excess of needs or possible uses, while
others are destitute of consuming power enough to satisfy
even the full demands of physical efficiency" (Hobson,
1971:83).

Hobson believed that the necessity for markets and in-
vestment-outlets did not make imperial expansion unavoidable. The fallacy of this belief therefore had to be exposed.
He argued that the expansion of industry per se does not
lead to overinvestment and overproduction and, hence, to
imperialism. Rather, "monopoly profits, and other unearned
or excessive elements of income [and the other side of the
coin] mal-distribution of consuming power . . . prevents
the absorption of commodities and capital within the country" (Hobson, 1971:85).

In these terms, Hobson was vehemently anti-imperial-
ist, advocating fundamental social reforms and peace, without which such reforms are impossible. Consistently raising
the living standards of the people would render imperialism
unnecessary. The destruction of human and natural resources resulting from war and militarism would be sup-

planted by a full employment of capital and labor intelligently allocated to meet the wants and needs of all. The difficulties of all capitalist economies in generating consumption for their commodities is attested to by recurrent crises and by the phenomenal growth of advertising and middlemen of all sorts. The root cause of this state of affairs is no mere temporary miscalculation or lack of adjustment. Rather, it is a general and chronic organized waste, a waste contained in the divorcement of the desire to consume and the power to consume. Hobson (1971:87) asserted that existing conditions could and must be changed and replaced by alternative economic arrangements in which the growing wants of the people "would be a constant stimulus to the inventive and operative energies of producers, and would form a constant strain upon the powers of production."

Therefore, a false and inequitable system of distribution had been the main source of the pathology. This system accounted for the unavailability of markets and investment outlets—hence, for imperial expansion and struggle among rivals. There was a remedy: social reform and peace. Therefore,

> the only safety of nations lies in removing the unearned increments of income from the possessing classes, and adding them to the wage-income of the working classes or to the public income, in order that they may be spent in raising the standard of consumption (Hobson, 1971:89).

In Hobson's view, the trade union and socialist movements are the natural enemies of imperialism insofar as they strive to institute these reforms. Recognizing this, the imperialist interests resolutely oppose reforms and try to crush or control the trade union movement.

Hobson did not think that the international peace and social reforms he advocated would be politically easy to realize. He wanted to prove the validity of his economic theory in order to dispel what he regarded as the dangerous illusion that imperial expansion and rivalry, with all that these imply, are the only possible outcome of the stage of industrial capitalism at that time.

Time and again, Hobson emphasized that the driving force behind imperialism is a definite class interest. He recognized clearly that no real change can be effected as long as this force is left intact:

> It is idle to attack Imperialism or Militarism as political expedients or policies unless the axe is laid at the economic root of the tree, and the classes for whose interest Imperialism works are shorn of the surplus revenues which seek this outlet (Hobson, 1971:93).

Hobson believed that the economic root could be cut even while capitalism prevailed. Political pressures of the working and other classes whose interests had been damaged and ill-served by imperialism were capable of bringing about the needed social reforms.

CAPITALISM AND IMPERIALISM

There is nothing equivocal about Hobson's analysis. It is forthright throughout. A variety of vested interests, mainly capitalist, used the governmental machinery to secure economic advantages both at home and in the colonies. These vested interests dominated public policy, particularly as it related to taxation and government expenditures. The undeniable results were the vast (over two-thirds) and growing proportions of the national budget for military purposes, including naval armament and equipment. These expenditures had grown faster than total expenditures had increased and, in fact, faster than had the increase of trade and of national income. These sums had been exacted from the national wealth by the financial and industrial classes who formed the core of the imperialist interest and continally sought "to improve their investments and open up new fields for capital, and to find profitable markets for their surplus [goods while out of the public sums] expended on these objects they reap other great private gains in the shape of profitable contracts (Hobson, 1971:95–96).

While the capitalist-imperialist classes constituted the pivot of imperial financial policy and benefited most directly from it, not all the other classes failed to gain from the policy. In a passage that anticipates Lenin's conception of the "labor aristocracy" and, at the same time, bears at least some resemblance to the present situation in the United States, Hobson (1971:97) wrote:

> While the directors of this definitely parasitic policy are capitalists, the same motives appeal to special classes of the workers. In many towns most important trades are dependent upon Government employment or contracts; . . . Members of Parliament freely employ their influence to secure contracts and direct trade to their constituents, and every growth of public expenditure enhances this dangerous bias.

Correspondingly,

> Popular education, instead of serving as a defense, is an incitement towards Imperialism; it has opened up a panorama of vulgar pride and crude sensationalism to a great inert mass who see current history and the tangled maze of world movements with dim, bewildered eyes, and are the inevitable dupes of the able organised interests who can lure, or scare, or drive them into any convenient course (Hobson, 1971:101).

Imperialist policy was therefore rooted in the interests of powerful and well-organized financial and industrial groups who successfully enlist the state to secure and develop markets and investment outlets for their surplus goods and surplus capital. Although the goals of imperialism were accomplished at public expense and involved the people in war, militarism, and the continual risks that an aggressive foreign policy entails, substantial ranks of the people supported the imperialist policy either because they derived some immediate material advantage from it or because they were carried away by a vulgar and emotional nationalism.

As for the great majority of the colonial peoples, they were not only economically exploited, but politically oppressed. The two went together of course. Throughout the empire, British rulers prevented the people from developing any real powers of self-government. The people enjoyed neither political power nor civil liberties, and the rulers had no intention of granting these colonials either the rights of British citizenship or the rights of citizens of self-governing, independent nations.

Thus, imperialism imposed a condition of servitude, of despotism, on the people of colonial empires. Indeed, imperialism is the very antithesis of the liberal credo—peace, freedom, economy—and brings with it horrendous consequences for peoples of the dominating and dominated countries alike.

> The decades of Imperialism have been prolific in wars; most of these wars have been directly motivated by aggression of white races upon "lower races," and have issued in the forcible seizure of territory. Every one of the steps of expansion in Africa, Asia, and the Pacific has been accompanied by bloodshed; each imperialist power keeps an increasing army available for foreign service; rectification of frontiers, punitive expeditions, and other euphemisms for war have been in incessant progress (Hobson, 1971:126).

In addition to the destruction wrought by wars, a permanent militarism drained the resources and sapped the energies of the European peoples, in spite of the fact that their interests were not served by the conflict. On the contrary, the so-called national antagonisms actually were of a "business nature. . . . only the interests of competing cliques of business men . . . are antagonistic"; they are the ones who drove the people into "this vast and disastrous military game, feigning national antagonisms which have no basis in reality" (Hobson, 1971:127). But there is just no getting around this situation as long as imperialism pre-

vailed, for it necessarily "implies militarism now and ruin-
ous wars in the future" (Hobson, 1971:130). The slaughter
of one's fellow men is the ghastly consequence of imperial
rivalry and the militarism accompanying it.

Within the imperialist country itself, sometimes euphe-
mistically called the mother country, there was therefore a
definite antagonism between the interest of the imperialists
and the interests of the people—whether the latter appreci-
ated this fact or not. As long as vast resources were wasted
on ever-increasing military expenditures, these resources
were unavailable for important social purposes. Moreover,
imperialism reinforced and safeguarded property, power,
and privilege, using "national animosities, foreign wars and
the glamour of empire-making, in order to bemuse the popular mind and divert rising resentment against domestic
abuses" (Hobson, 1971:142). As a result, whatever little
control the people might have over policy was further diminished. In Parliament, the ability of the opposition to
resist was progressively reduced, while real power was concentrated in an "inner Cabinet." And insofar as no effective
opposition exists, "the only real political conflict is between
groups representing the divergent branches of Imperialism"
(Hobson, 1971:149).

What chance was there of changing this state of
affairs? Hobson perceived a distinct possibility, as did
Lenin after him, "that the body of the workers in different
countries who fight and pay for wars would refuse to fight
and pay in the future if they were allowed to understand
the real nature of the issues used to inflame them" (Hobson,
1971:170). Failure of policies promoting true internationalism and peace indicated "the presence in high places of
cliques and classes opposed in their interests and feelings
to those of the people, and the necessity of dethroning these
enemies of the people if the new cause of internationalism
is to advance. Secure popular government, in substance and
in form, and you secure internationalism: retain class government, and you retain military Imperialism and international conflicts" (Hobson, 1971:171).

Nor did it escape Hobson (1971:174) as early as the

turn of the century, that the "bleeding of dependencies . . . irritates and eventually rouses to rebellion the more vigorous and less tractable of the subject races."

Also clear was that the hegemony of the imperialist groups at home was made possible by a systematic masking of hard facts. Before they could mislead the people, the leaders often found it necessary first to mislead themselves. Through the distortion of reality, both conscious and unconscious, the imperialist ideology became so prevalent that all domestic criticism of imperialism was attributed to an antipatriotic bias.

The process of diffusing the imperialist ideology began with certain financial and industrial sections of the capitalist class whose interests in imperialism were material and direct. These sections enlisted the active cooperation of political leaders and cliques either by involving them in their businesses or by appealing to their conservative sentiments as members of the propertied and privileged classes. Politicians were easily persuaded that the diversion of public attention from domestic to foreign politics would best preserve their common vested interests and class domination. As for the masses, they were won over by deceit—a falsification of the true nature of war and imperial policy—and a stimulation of the primitive emotions and ideas associated with Jingoism.

The press, schools, colleges, and the church all participated in this falsification. Considering the recent history of conflict and controversy in American universities, it is interesting that Hobson recognized the influence of imperialism on higher education. "The centres of highest culture, the universities, are in peril of a new perversion from the path of free inquiry and expression" (Hobson, 218). Not that the academic establishment and teachers, succumbing to business and political pressures, consciously twisted the truth, particularly in such disciplines as history, economics, and sociology, "but the actual teaching is none the less selected and controlled. . . . No one can follow the history of political and economic theory during the last century without recognizing that the selection and rejection of ideas, hypotheses, and formulae, the moulding of them into schools or tendencies of thought, and the propagation of them in the intellectual world, have been plainly directed by the pressure of class interests" (Hobson, 1971:218).

In universities, in elementary and high schools, in the press and from the pulpit, a definite deference to the imperialist ideology was evident. The voices that called into question the dominant policy were too few and too weak to expose the so-called civilizing mission of the white man for what it was: a smoke screen behind which the cheap labor of dependent and colonial subjects could be employed "in developing the resources of their own lands under white control for white men's profit" (Hobson, 1971:249). Whether on plantations, in mines, or in factories, the people were subjected to a system of forced labor i.e., "labour which natives would not undertake save under direct or indirect personal compulsion issuing from white masters" (Hobson, 1971:254). With their land and other resources confiscated and their traditional agrarian life destroyed, colonials were effectively transformed into a servile class.

When Hobson speaks of the "parasitic" character of imperialism, this is no mere phrase. Rather, it is a precise term referring to exploitation in an objective sense. Everywhere, the relation of the European to the native is exploitative; nowhere is it based on a "balance of mutual services" (Hobson, 1971:282). That the relation of the white rulers is distinctively parasitic may be seen in the fact that, everywhere, they imposed a regime that would ensure "the profitable development of certain natural resources of the land, under 'forced' native labour, primarily for the benefit of the white traders and investors, and secondarily for the benefit of the world of white Western consumers" (Hobson, 1971: 283).

For the people of the imperialist countries, this policy was also costly and tragic. It involved them in wars, wasted precious resources, and diverted attention from their real human needs which, as a result, remained unmet. But for colonial people who had been forcibly subjected to an unchecked parasitism, it was even more costly and tragic—

however much imperialism's apologists may protest to the contrary. Indeed, the pretense that the imperial country was rendering a service to the subjugated peoples implied "a degree of moral or intellectual obliquity so grave as itself to form a new peril for any nation fostering so false a notion of the nature of its conduct" (Hobson, 1971:368).

Ultimately, the people could rid themselves of imperialism in only one way: by overthrowing the old government and supplanting it with a genuine democracy. Whether any of the imperial nations were ready for so fundamental a change was a "matter of grave doubt, but until and unless the external policy of a nation is 'broad-based upon a people's will' there appears little hope of remedy" (Hobson, 1971:360–361).

This is an adequate outline of Hobson's analysis, the main elements of which Lenin elaborated and incorporated into his own Marxian framework.

7

Lenin's Theory

Hobson had seen clearly that far from being a form of peaceful economic competition, imperialist rivalry and the domination of peoples were inescapably bound up with war and the preparation for war. If this was clear to Hobson in 1902, little wonder that it was even clearer to Lenin (1939) in 1916, when he wrote his critique of imperialism.

For Lenin, writing in the midst of the First World War, there could be no doubt that this war was the most destructive and tragic manifestation of the struggle for the division, or more correctly the redivision, of the world. The war was annexationist and predatory, a struggle for the "partition and repartition of colonies, 'spheres of influence' of finance capital, etc." (Lenin, 1939:9). In this sense, the same as Hobson's, the war was *imperialistic* for Lenin. The people of Europe had been led by their imperialist governments into the war of 1914–18; the terrible cost of this war was tens of millions of dead and mutilated humans who had been sacrificed to determine whether British or German financial-industrial groups would dominate the colonial world. Would the British retain their markedly advantageous position or would the Germans upset it, gaining for themselves a more favorable share of the spoils?

And why assume, Lenin argued, that this would be the last of such destructive and tragic wars? Assume that, in fact, the underlying causes were the contradiction between the immense productivity of social production and private property in the means of production; the concentration and accumulation of capital proceeding at a rapid rate; the financial-industrial oligarchies in each advanced capitalist country that successfully employed the political and military power of the state to secure spheres of interest; and adequate markets and profitable investment outlets that continued to be urgent for these oligarchies. If, in a word, advanced capitalism should continue to prevail in several countries that continued to compete for sources of cheap raw material, markets, and investment opportunities, what grounds were there for assuming that imperialist wars would not occur in the future?

In these terms, "imperialism" and "monopoly capital" are not catchwords for Lenin, but scientific, analytical concepts. As long as the structure and tendencies of monopoly capital remained in effect, that structure could be expected to conduce in the future to processes and events much like those of the past. Under these objective circumstances, there simply was no solid ground for assuming that the interests and policies of the ruling financial and industrial groups would change fundamentally.

Therefore, when Lenin asserted that as long as monopoly capital prevails, imperialist wars are inevitable, he was not merely creating catchwords and phrases for propaganda purposes. Nor was this proposition intended as dogma. On the contrary, he was presenting a proposition derived from what he considered to be a scientifically accurate analysis of the master trends of a historically specific social system.

Lenin began his essay by drawing attention to one of

the most important of the master trends: the rapid concentration of production into ever larger enterprises. We considered much of what Lenin said in this connection earlier, in our review of the early history of monopoly formation. This discussion will not be repeated here. For our purposes, a summary of the main argument is sufficient.

Following mainly Hobson and Hilferding, but employing other sources as well, Lenin showed that the characteristic feature of all advanced capitalist countries is the trend toward monopoly. Many economists acknowledged and described this fact. But some of them, Marxists included, drew conclusions that Lenin regarded as false and dangerous insofar as the people and their leaders believed them. Some economists argued that because monopoly was superseding competition, capitalism was achieving the ability to regulate production, to overcome its planlessness, and to abolish crises. Lenin regards these contentions as a dangerous fallacy, for there could be no doubt that monopoly intensified "the anarchy inherent in capitalist production *as a whole*" (Lenin, 1939:28). Concerted action and coordination in some industries or branches of production were accompanied by the lack of coordination in others. Conflicts of interest and rivalry prevailed among capitalist groups. Moreover, economic crises continued to accompany concentration and monopoly. But the concentration of industrial production alone did not account for the centralization of economic power. Banks and other financial institutions now played a key role in the process.

The unprecedentedly large scale of industrial production that became characteristic of capitalism with the second industrial revolution showed that producers now needed immense sums of money capital for the huge outlays production required. Seldom were industrialists able to generate this capital themselves; more and more, they depended on bankers and financiers. The concentration of production continued to parallel the centralization of banking and finance capital. Small banks were pushed aside or swallowed up by big ones, and a few powerful banks soon acquired control of industry. These powerful banks knew precisely the financial status of a few large industrial and other business undertakings. By facilitating or hindering the extension of credit, the banks could determine the fate of these businesses. The power of the banks was further enhanced by the state's dependence on them for subsidizing certain industrial developments and financing militarization. This general process became evident at the turn of the century. Rudolf Hilferding (1968) analyzed the process in detail in his aptly entitled book, *Das Finanzkapital*. Finance capital, as Hilferding and Lenin understood and used the term, referred to the central tendencies of the new stage of capitalism: accelerated industrial concentration; oligopoly and monopoly in both industry and finance; and the merging of banking and industry.

THE LAW OF UNEVEN DEVELOPMENT

Another characteristic of the new stage of capitalism was the accumulation of a superabundance of capital in all the advanced industrial countries. Because England had the first industrial revolution, she became the "workshop of the world." Selling manufactured goods to others and buying raw materials in turn, she remained the most powerful industrial country in the world well beyond the mid-nineteenth century. As long as she remained the most advanced, she was able to undersell all others and the doctrine of free trade was therefore definitely to her interest. By the last quarter of the nineteenth century, however, several countries threatened England's hegemony. By rejecting free trade and protecting their infant industries with high tariff walls, Germany, the United States, France, and Japan increasingly undermined England's economic position and grew to be powerful industrial states.

The long-time dominance of England and the *industrial* catching up and surpassing of England by others was a manifestation of what Lenin called the law of uneven development under capitalism. The law referred to the un-evenness of development among branches of industry, among industries, and among national economies. Begin-ning in the last few decades of the nineteenth century and gathering momentum in the twentieth century, an acceler-ated tendency toward capital concentration and oligopoly *within* each capitalist country manifested itself at the same time as a few of these advanced capitalist states achieved outstanding industrial power in the world economy. Hobson had described this situation as a few industrial powers vying among themselves for markets and investment out-lets for their surplus commodities and capital. Lenin had no quarrel with Hobson's analysis, but he disagreed with Hobson's conclusion.

To be sure, Hobson himself had insisted that imperial-ism could never be abolished without removing the ruling imperialist elements from power and establishing a genuine democracy. Although he never discussed in detail the politi-cal means by which this change could be accomplished, Hobson apparently believed that such far-reaching changes could be brought about through parliamentary reforms. Re-forms would raise the living standards of the great masses and absorb the economic surplus, thus, striking at the eco-nomic taproot of imperialism. "But," Lenin (1939:63) ob-jected,

> if capitalism did these things it would not be capi-talism; for uneven development and wretched conditions of the masses are fundamental and in-evitable conditions and premises of the mode of production. As long as capitalism remains what it is, surplus capital will never be utilised for the purpose of raising the standard of living of the masses in a given country, for this would mean a decline of profits for the capitalists; it will be used for the purpose of increasing those profits by ex-porting capital abroad to the backward countries. In these backward countries profits are usually high, for capital is scarce, the price of land is rela-tively low, wages are low, raw materials are cheap.

Indeed, the available data showed that Britain's, Germany's, and France's export of capital increased continuously from the 1860s until World War I. Britain's principal investments were in her colonies and in Canada and the United States. France limited hers mainly to investments in Europe, notably in Russia in the form of government loans and not of investments in industrial undertakings. As for Germany, who had only a few colonial possessions, her foreign investments were "divided fairly evenly between Europe and America" (Lenin, 1939:65).

Thus, a few capitalist states dominated and divided the world among themselves. But the older, colonizing states such as Britain and France still held the lion's share, and German capitalists envied the older established imperialist powers just as the United States capital interests envied both the old and the new. Britain possessed a vast colonial empire, while Germany had captured a relatively minute share; nevertheless, Germany recently had achieved superior industrial strength. These inequities were a major source of the tension between the two powers that eventually exploded in 1914.

A partition of the entire world market by a handful of industrial powers accompanied the division of the home market by a few giant financial and industrial groups. Especially where price competition threatened to be mutually destructive, risky, or costly, expediency dictated formation of international agreements among the few giants of the various capitalist countries. Hence, the era of international cartels.

The formation of cartels did not dispel rivalry and competition once and for all. In various industries, notably oil, the struggle for the *redivision* of the world market continued and even intensified (for example, in the years immediately preceding the First World War, the struggle first between the Rockefeller and Anglo-Dutch Shell trusts and later between the victorious Rockefeller trust and the Deutsche Bank, resulting in the defeat of the latter).

At the same time, the great capitalist states had completed their division of the colonial world among themselves.

The period between approximately 1860 and 1900 was characterized by accomplishment of the "final partition of the globe. . . . Not in the sense that a *new* partition is impossible—on the contrary, new partitions are possible and inevitable—but in the sense that the colonial policy of the capitalist countries has *completed* the seizure of the unoccupied territories on our planet. [Since the world is already divided] *only* redivision is possible; territories can only pass from one 'owner' to another, instead of passing as unowned territory to an 'owner' " (Lenin, 1939:76).

Clearly, then, the great upsurge in colonial expansion begins in the period *after* competitive capitalism has reached its zenith and the

> struggle for the territorial division of the world becomes extraordinarily keen. It is beyond doubt, therefore, that capitalism's transition to the stage of monopoly capitalism, to finance capital, is *bound up* with the intensification of the struggle for the partition of the World (Lenin, 1939: 77–78).

Therefore, the relationship between monopoly capital and imperialism was inescapable. In 1876, three powers—Germany, the United States, and Japan—had no colonial possessions and a fourth—France—had only a few. By 1914, these four powers had acquired "14,100,000 square kilometres of colonies, or an area one and a half times greater than that of Europe" (Lenin, 1939:80).

Yet the rate of colonial expansion among these powers and the magnitude of their colonial possessions was conspicuously uneven. For instance, France had annexed almost three times as much colonial territory as had Germany and Japan combined; France also was considerably richer in finance capital than were Germany and Japan together. At the same time, the industrial development of the advanced capitalist countries was uneven. On one side, although the older powers of Great Britain and France, possessed the lion's share of the colonies, they had slowed down industrially. On the other side, the young and vigorous capitalisms of United States, Germany, and Japan were developing quite rapidly, although they were poor in colonies. Under these circumstances, rivalry, conflicts, and even war among the imperialist powers appeared almost inevitable.

Another important point is that there are various forms of dependence. This will be apparent later in another context. Some countries retain their political sovereignty, or a semblance thereof, but are nonetheless so financially dependent on advanced capitalist countries that they constitute semi- or quasi-colonies. Examples of such countries are found today in Latin America and in other parts of the underdeveloped world. On the other hand, imperialism also strives to dominate and control highly industrialized countries.

IMPERIALISM AS A SPECIAL STAGE OF CAPITALISM

Beginning in the latter half of the nineteenth century, an accelerated concentration of production, particularly in those countries that experienced the second industrial revolution, gave rise to oligopoly and monopoly that increasingly supplanted competitive capitalism. The qualitatively larger scale of production that was becoming typical required sums of capital so vast that seldom could industrialists generate them without borrowing from the banks. Banks loaned capital under conditions that enabled them to gain a controlling interest of industry. Industrial and bank capital merged to form a powerful financial-industrial oligarchy in the economic world. The accumulation of unprecedentedly large capital surpluses that found no profitable investment at home was a concomitant of these developments. Capital was exported with an increasing frequency and magnitude. Among the industrial and financial giants of the advanced capitalist countries, cartel and other type agreements were entered into as a means of exercising monopoly power over the supply and price of their products. Finally, the advanced capitalist powers extended their sway over the entire non-capitalist and partially capitalist world. With division of the colonial and dependent world thus completed, the imperialist powers continued their struggle for the *redivision* of that world.

This summary should clarify the historical and theoretical considerations that led Lenin to define imperialism as "the monopoly stage of capitalism." In these terms, imperial expansion was no mere policy, as Karl Kautsky and other Marxists had maintained. For Kautsky, imperialism was a policy in the sense that militarism, expansion, and the domination of colonies was *not* inevitably bound up with monopoly capital and finance-capital hegemony. Imperialism was a policy in that certain interest groups preferred it to other policies.

Lenin vehemently rejected Kautsky's view as misleading and unMarxian—misleading because it necessitated the belief that contemporary capitalism was capable of becoming nonexpansionist and nonmilitaristic and unMarxian because it severed the politics of imperialism from the very economic conditions that generated it. In short, Lenin criticized Kautsky for fostering the impression that imperialist politics could be eliminated without striking at its economic roots. Indeed, from this angle, Kautsky the Marxist understood less than Hobson, the liberal reformist, had. For as we have already seen, Hobson (1971:93) plainly had recognized that "it is idle to attack Imperialism or Militarism as political expedients unless the axe is laid at the economic root of the tree, and the classes for whose interest Imperialism works are shorn of the surplus revenues which seek this outlet."

Lenin also disagreed with Kautsky's positing of a new phase, conceived on the eve of World War I, toward which capitalism was purportedly developing—a peaceful phase he called "ultra-imperialism" in which a union of the various national financial-industrial oligarchies would exploit the world without militarism and war. Kautsky's ultra-imperialism thus assumed that the new capitalism would somehow do away with the law of uneven development and other basic conflicts of interest. This view flew in the face of empirical historical facts.

By way of illustration, Lenin pointed briefly to the increasing acuteness in the developing struggle for Latin America; to the mounting intensity of the conflict between the United States and Japan; and, generally, to the conflict between the old established imperial powers and the new ones. As we already have seen, England was the most advanced of the industrial societies when she founded her empire. Eventually, she fell behind the United States and Germany in spite of the fact that these two countries were more industrially advanced, but possessed no colonies to further their economic interests. Thus, while Britain and France lagged industrially behind Germany and the United States, the former powers maintained enormously advantageous positions throughout the colonial world. From the end of the nineteenth century until the outbreak of World War I, Britain's industrial production and foreign trade developed less rapidly than Germany's did. While Germany was capable of underselling Britain in the world market, her exports to the colonies were only a small fraction of Britain's.

Lenin provided some of the relevant statistics and asked: "[I]s there *under capitalism* any means of removing the disparity between the development of productive forces and the accumulation of capital on the one side, and the division of colonies and 'spheres of influence' for finance capital on the other side—other than by resorting to war?" (Lenin, 1939:98).

Writing during a period of war and revolution, Lenin perceived Kautsky's and all other similar doctrines as "opportunistic." By this term, Lenin meant that labor leaders who put forward such analyses and doctrines were consciously or unconsciously expressing the interests not of the masses of working people, but only of an upper stratum that he dubbed the "labor aristocracy." This stratum derived definite material advantages from imperialism and therefore tended to support imperial interests.

This phenomenon was not new. In mid-nineteenth century, when Britain occupied a monopoly position in the world market, Frederick Engels (Marx and Engels, 1953a: 123–33) complained of certain labor leaders whose conduct, he believed, was

> bound up with the fact that the English proletariat is actually becoming more and more bourgeois, so that the most bourgeois of all nations is apparently aiming ultimately at the possession of a bourgeois aristocracy and a bourgeois proletariat *alongside* the bourgeoisie. For a nation which exploits the whole world this is of course to a certain extent justifiable.

Engels expressed himself similarly in a number of occasions in the ensuing years. In his 1892 preface to *The Condition of the Working Class in England,* he used the term "working-class aristocracy" and reaffirmed the analysis he had made earlier:

> During the period of England's industrial monopoly the English working class have, to a certain extent, shared in the benefits of the monopoly. These benefits were very unequally parcelled out amongst them; the privileged minority pocketed the most, but even the great mass had, at least, a temporary share now and then. And that is the reason why, since the dying out of Owenism, there has been no Socialism in England (Marx and Engels, 1953b:30–31).

Thus for Engels, as later for Lenin, there were sound reasons why the imperialist ideology could not fail but to penetrate at least the upper strata of the working class.[1] However, Lenin may very well have *underestimated* the scope and depth of this ideological penetration. We shall touch on some of the implications of this error later.

Our brief review of Lenin's *Imperialism* has shown

---

[1] For Lenin's references to the "labor aristocracy" and related ideas, see *Imperialism* (1939:13, 104, 106–107, 109 and 126).

quite plainly how he built on Hobson's work and integrated it with Marxism. Before we ask whether this theory of imperialism applies to some of the present-day relations of the United States with other countries and, if so, in what degree and manner, there are other implications of the theory that deserve to be mentioned, if only briefly.

8

Further Implications
of the Hobson-Lenin Theory

Modern imperialism differs from previous forms in a number of important respects. In earlier forms, the imperial powers most often contented themselves with plundering their colonies or establishing a system for exacting continual tribute. One important motive was the lust for "treasure." Precious metals such as gold and silver and jewels such as diamonds, rubies, and pearls were taken from weaker peoples either by force or by fraud.

Another important motive was the desire to acquire slave labor. Hobson (1971:247), for example, reminds us that "the earliest, the most profitable trade in the history of the world has been the slave trade." Greek and Roman imperialists established settlements among the conquered for the purpose of securing the payment of tribute as well as an assured source of slave labor, that the conquerors brought back to their own countries. In these terms, the economies of the conquered or dominated underwent no fundamental change.

In contrast, modern imperialism does in fact undermine the colonial economy: slaves are replaced by wage-laborers or the like, who are employed in extracting and working up the natural resources of their own lands, which are under imperialist control for imperialist profit. Capitalist imperialism cannot be satisfied merely with exacting tribute. It must establish industries for the extraction of natural resources and organize markets for its commodities, both of which lead to a substantial transformation of the colonial economic system.

The self-sufficient economies of the Asian peasants, for example, provided no market for capitalist industry. Imperialism therefore transformed these economies. At the same time that it destroyed the native handicraft industry of great masses of peasants, it built harbors and large networks of railways to bring its products into the colonial market. Colonial peoples were thus compelled to purchase the industrial commodities of the "mother" country and in general became increasingly dependent on it.

In some ways, the destruction of the traditional methods of production of the colonial areas paralleled the process that had taken place a few generations earlier in the imperialist countries themselves. But there was one essential difference: the domination of the industrially undeveloped regions by the advanced capitalist-industrial powers resulted in only a limited industrialization of the colonies. Imperial domination not only destroyed or undermined the colonies' original economies, but led to a partial and lopsided industrialization as well. That this would be the ultimate consequence of imperial rule was not generally suspected during the early phases of imperial expansion.

Even Marx, an exceptionally thorough student of capitalism, failed to foresee this consequence. He believed that British construction of railways in India would unavoidably lead to India's industrialization to the point where the colony eventually would mirror the mother country. In an article entitled "The Future Results of British Rule in

India" and published in the *New York Daily Tribune* on July 22, 1853, Marx (1853) wrote:

> I know that the English millocracy intend to endow India with railways with the exclusive view of extracting at diminished expenses the cotton and other raw materials for their manufactures. But when you have once introduced machinery into the locomotion of a country, which possesses iron and coals, you are unable to withhold it from its fabrication. You cannot maintain a net of railways over an immense country without introducing all those industrial processes necessary to meet the immediate and current wants of railway locomotion, and out of which there must grow the application of machinery to those branches of industry not immediately connected with railways. *The railway system will therefore become, in India, truly the forerunner of modern industry* [italics added].[1]

Marx's expectations were never fulfilled, either in India or in any other colonial area, for it became a cardinal principle of every imperialist's policy to prevent and retard industrial development in the colonies. Had these colonies been allowed a full and unhampered industrialization, they would have become economically independent, an eventuality clearly antagonistic to imperial interests.

 But the imperialist policy was motivated by political considerations as well. Fully industrializing the colonies would have given rise to both an indigenous capitalist class and a large class of industrial workers. Experience had shown that, even in their embryonic growth, these classes developed a national consciousness and became a major source of opposition to imperial domination. Perpetuation of imperial rule therefore dictated a policy of permitting colonial industrialization, in kind and degree, only insofar as it appeared compatible with imperial interests.

To achieve this goal and to ensure domination of the colonies, imperialists, vastly outnumbered by the colonial

[1] See also Christman (1966:106–7).

population in every colony, sought allies among them. Typically, the most important of these allies were the landlords. By bolstering the privileges of this class and fostering its development even where it was weak, the imperialists gained the support of a powerful class of rich landed proprietors who were vitally interested in imperialism and capable of controlling the popular masses. This alliance made mass poverty the normal condition of the people. For on the one hand, their misery was perpetuated by industrial stagnation and, on the other, by an imperialist-landlord alliance that made anything but the most superficial of agrarian reforms unthinkable.

In sharp contrast to the bourgeoisie's history in Europe, where it fought and opposed the feudal classes, the imperial bourgeoisie deliberately perpetuated landlordism in the colonies. Of course, the imperialist-landlord alliance contributed further to the economic stagnation of the colonies because both groups had a powerful interest in preventing industrialization and the profound structural changes that inevitably would follow. Yet no one foresaw the long-term boomerang effect that this alliance and the accompanying policy would have on the economies of the mother capitalist countries.

In the early period of imperial expansion, the destruction of native handicraft industries, together with the construction of railways, definitely provided the mother countries with growing markets. In the later period of imperial domination, however, the situation changed fundamentally. Completion of the railway network and the thorough ruination of the great mass of handicraft workers coupled with the deliberate policy of assuring industrial stagnation in the colonies converged to fix the living standards of hundreds of millions of people in the colonies at so low a level that they ceased to constitute an adequate market.

Actually, of course, this is an understatement. It would be far more accurate to say that the great masses of the colonial and semicolonial areas lived under the continual threat of starvation. In his well-known study, Colin Clark (1940) sought to compare the standards of living of the peoples of the world. Toward this end Clark (1940:2) developed a unit of measure that he called an "International Unit," defined as "the amount of goods and services which could be purchased for one dollar in the United States on an average throughout the decade 1925–34."

It is highly instructive to compare the living standards as measured by international units per capita per year in the advanced capitalist countries with those in the colonial world. The United States, Canada, and Great Britain, for example, enjoyed standards of 1300 to 1400, 1200 to 1300, and 1000 to 1100 international units, respectively. At the other extreme, more than half of the world's population at the time (1,113 million out of a total of 2,095 million) struggled for survival at a level below 200 international units. The vast majority of the severely impoverished half of the human race lived under imperialist domination in the colonial and dependent areas of the world.

While impoverishment became more severe among the colonial peoples, the real wages of workers in the capitalistically advanced countries continued to rise. Up until the great crisis that began in 1929, there seems to have been a definite relationship between the rising living standards in the industrially advanced countries and the imperialist exploitation of the colonial and semicolonial areas. In these terms, imperialism, as well as the expansion of capitalism itself, particularly in the United States, served to diminish the tensions among social classes in the capitalist societies of Europe.

Earlier, we saw that Lenin, following Engels, had attempted to explain what he regarded as the opportunistic-reformist tendencies of the European labor movement on the basis of a so-called "labor aristocracy" that had emerged in the imperialist countries. But if real wages of industrial workers continued to rise in the European imperialist countries up to the outbreak of the First World War, Lenin may have erred in believing that only a slender stratum of workers gained higher material standards of living from imperial domination. This erroneous assumption probably accounts for his anticipation of socialist revolutions in western

Europe—particularly during World War I and the Russian Revolutions of 1917, and even for a few years afterward. As we have seen, Lenin firmly believed that imperialism was the highest or last stage of capitalism.

Today we know definitely that no social revolution has occurred in, any of the advanced capitalist countries.

We also know that since Lenin's time, mankind has experienced a second world war, more devastating than the first. In the period following that war, a variety of factors contributed to the success of social revolutions and national independence movements throughout the colonial and dependent world. Imperialism seemed to have been throttled once and for all. At the same time, the United States emerged as the most powerful state in the world. Some serious people argue that the United States has in fact become the chief imperialist power today. However, the form its domination of others has assumed differs in important respects from the form described by Hobson and Lenin. How does it differ? This is the question to which we now turn.

dependency today?

The earlier imperialism we have so far been considering was an expansionist movement in which several advanced capitalist countries participated. Undoubtedly, the United States was among them. The economic forces impelling her in that direction were not unlike those at work in the other capitalist countries: inadequate markets and investment outlets for an increasingly powerful industrial apparatus. The giant United States industrialists and financiers turned their eyes to the Pacific, to China, to Latin America. Striving for control of these areas as exclusive as possible in order to secure them against the competition of Britain, Germany, and others, the United States succeeded in establishing political control of the areas she most prized. Cuba, the Philippines, and Hawaii are the most obvious examples.

Of course, United States expansionism did not begin in this period. It was given merely a renewed and powerful impetus. Throughout most of the nineteenth century, and quite apart from its expansion on the American Continent, the United States played the role of Britain's junior partner, always exacting the highest price possible for her support. By the turn of the nineteenth century, the United States had not only actively built an empire, but, under provisions of the Monroe Doctrine, also had laid claim to a far larger domain.

The renewed impetus to her expansion came in the late nineteenth century and coincided with the second industrial revolution, increased protectionism, and the emergence of monopoly capital. By the beginning of the First World War, the imperial possessions of the United States were sufficient to make of her a "have" power, and she joined Britain and France against the leading contenders. Her power grew continually thereafter, at the expense of both allies and enemies, and she emerged from the Second World War as the unquestioned leader of the capitalist world.

But the years following that war brought with them some far-reaching changes. The western European capitalist countries found themselves weak and exhausted. In addition, capitalism had been extinguished not only in the Soviet Union, but also in eastern Europe[2] and, soon afterward, in China. Elsewhere, capitalism underwent a significant transformation. At the same time and subsequently, nationalist, anticolonial, and other revolutionary movements weakened and broke up the European colonial empires. As a result, while the capitalist world had been severely contracted and the older colonial empires liquidated, the United States emerged as the only power that could successfully fill the vacuum created by the collapse of European and Japanese colonialism. Moreover, she was the only power that could lead and help both western Europe and Japan to economic recovery on a capitalist basis.

In an era when capitalism was substantially contracting and the older colonial domination was being shaken off,

[2] To avoid any possible misunderstanding, I want to emphasize that I intend this as a purely descriptive statement. Hence, it should not be taken to mean that I believe that the so-called socialist systems are necessarily good societies or that they are inevitably superior ethically and humanly to all capitalist systems.

the hegemony of the United States carried with it certain unavoidable implications. It now fell to this chief capitalist power to bear the primary responsibility for securing capitalism in western Europe, Latin America, and elsewhere. This she accomplished by curbing and, wherever possible, destroying any and all forces that threatened to deprive her of market and investment opportunities. Abandoning even the semblance of isolationism, the United States embarked on a policy of containment and eventually formed a host of treaties and agreements of which NATO, SEATO, and CENTO are only a few of the best known.

Accompanying this development was the unceasing expansion of the military establishment in the United States— an establishment that continues to grow today and threatens to become a permanent aspect of American social life.

At this time, the terrible war in Indo-China rages on. The destruction inflicted on the people, their works, and their environment staggers the imagination. In several other instances, the United States has intervened, directly or indirectly, in the internal affairs of other countries in an effort to influence and control their domestic and foreign policies. Therefore, the question that merits serious consideration is whether the United States foreign policy is determined largely by capitalist interests in markets, investment outlets, and sources of cheap raw material and labor. In short, is the United States today imperialistic?

9

The New Imperialism
of the United States

Military, industrial, and financial leadership of the capitalist world by the United States is presently so evident as to be beyond dispute. United States military bases may be found in every corner of the non-Socialist globe, tightly encircling and enclosing the Socialist countries.[1] By means of its military assistance and training programs, the United States has established a military presence, in one form or another, in at least 64 countries as compared with the 3 countries in which it had installations during the 1920s and the 39 [2]

[1] Again, I wish to remind the reader that I am using "Socialist" in this general context as a strictly descriptive term that official representatives of these countries employ to describe their social systems. My use of the term must not be construed to mean that I regard these systems as *necessarily* superior, in any human or ethical sense, to capitalist ones.

[2] In this discussion, I rely heavily on Harry Magdoff's (1969) thoroughly documented and well-argued study.

countries in which it maintained bases during World War II. United States armed forces are represented in 19 countries in Latin America, 10 in East Asia (including Australia), 11 in Africa, 13 in Europe, and 11 in the near East and South Asia combined (Magdoff, 1969:42).

At the same time, the United States has achieved the dominant position in international finance and in the control of strategic resources. The rich Middle-East oil reserves, for example, increasingly have come under the control of the United States. That this has been accompanied by the older imperialists' diminishing grip on these reserves is clear. In 1940, Great Britain, the United States, and other capitalist countries controlled some 72 percent, 9.8 percent, and 18.2 percent, respectively, of the reserves. By 1967, the figures were 29.3 percent, 58.6 percent, and 12.1 percent, respectively.

What remains as characteristic of United States imperialism as of the older forms is her reliance on external sources of raw materials. The monopoly position of the United States giant corporations as well as the volume of their profits have become more dependent on foreign sources than ever before. Indeed, more and more, the United States has become "a 'have-not' nation for a wide range of both common and rare minerals" (Magdoff, 1969:45). Nor is the increasing efficiency in the industrial use of raw materials likely to reverse this process, for as Magdoff (1969:46) observes, "no matter how efficient industry becomes in the use of aluminum [for example] or in the extraction of alumina from bauxite, you can't make aluminum without bauxite and you can't make an airplane without aluminum. And when in the United States, 80 to 90 percent of the bauxite supply comes from foreign sources, the assurance of such supply is of crucial importance to the aluminum industry, the airplane industry, and the country's military power."

The already powerful tendency of United States corporate giants to gain control of cheap, foreign sources of raw material is further intensified by the economy's growing dependence on foreign resources. If we use millions of 1954 dollars to compare the United States net imports of minerals with consumption, we find that in the period 1900–09, net imports, as a percentage of consumption, were: −1.5 percent; and that in the period 1910–19, they were −3.1—which means that in these years exports were larger than imports. Nevertheless, net imports increased to .7 percent of consumption in the period 1920–29, dipped slightly to .6 percent during the depression years (1930–39), jumped to 5.3 percent during the war years (1940–45) and rose continuously thereafter, reaching 14 percent in 1961 (U.S. Bureau of the Census, 1963).

It is perhaps not generally known that growing United States dependence on foreign resources applies to common and not merely to esoteric materials. For instance, United States net imports (as a percentage of domestic production) of iron ore, copper, lead, zinc, bauxite, and petroleum increased dramatically between 1937 and 1966. Magdoff (1969:48) calls attention particularly to the figures on iron ore. In the years just before the Second World War (1937–39), "net imports of iron ore amounted to about 3 percent of the close to 52 million tons of iron ore extracted from domestic sources. In 1966, net imports were equal to 43 percent of the 90 million tons mined in the country."

As one might have expected, the depletion of high-quality domestic ore led to a sharp increase "in foreign investment to develop more efficient and richer sources of iron ore in Canada, Venezuela, Brazil, and Africa. The purpose, as it developed, was not only to exploit more profitable sources of supply but to map out greater control over this essential raw material as a preventive measure: each large domestic producer naturally anticipates similar moves by other domestic and foreign producers" (Magdoff, 1969:49).

A large degree of dependence is similarly evident with respect to a host of vital and strategic materials—vital and strategic for civilian as well as for military production. The United States depends on imports for provision of 80–100 percent of more than half of some 62 such materials. As 75 percent of these materials are acquired from the underdeveloped countries, it is clear that U.S. dependence on these countries must be reflected in a large measure in its foreign policy. Whether the administration in Washington is Republican or Democratic, this dependence on underdeveloped areas governs the political and military actions of the United States in those areas.

THE UNITED STATES AS THE CHIEF EXPORTER OF CAPITAL

An important dimension of the older imperialisms, we will recall, was the export of capital, not merely commodities. Capital export is also an integral aspect of the U.S. economy. In fact, the United States is now the chief exporter of capital. This country's relative share of foreign investments increased from 6.3 percent in 1914 to 35.3 percent in 1930 to 59.1 percent in 1960—to almost 60 percent of the world total—and continued to increase during the 1960s. In the same period, the relative shares of Britain, France, and Germany declined sharply.

Available data on exports and sales from foreign investments are particularly useful in demonstrating that "by 1965, the sales of foreign affiliates are higher than exports from United-States based plants. More than that, the increase during these years [1957–65] has been larger in the case of foreign affiliates plants than in exports. For the industries combined, sales of foreign-owned plants rose 140 percent, while exports from the United States went up 55 percent" (Magdoff, 1969:58).

If we focus on foreign investment in *manufacturing,* we find that such investment is concentrated primarily in Canada and Europe. Since the end of the Second World War, U.S.-controlled firms have acquired a substantial and even a preponderant share of certain industries in Europe. One may get some idea of the extent of U.S. dominance from the fact that "United States firms control over half of the automobile industry in Britain, close to 40 percent of petroleum in Germany, and over 40 percent of the telegraphic, telephone, electronic, and statistical equipment business in France (the control of computing machines in France is 75 percent)" (Magdoff, 1969:60).

In this respect as in others, the new U.S. imperialism resembles the old. For as we saw earlier, an important feature of imperial policy is that it strives to dominate not only underdeveloped areas, but highly industrialized regions as well. What is different about the present-day domination of Europe by the United States is the *form* it has taken. The United States need not annex a country in order to acquire the high degree of economic control it has in fact achieved in western Europe.

Where is the connection between the already huge and growing U.S. investments in Europe and what we have called corporate or monopoly capitalism? Basing his observations on Christopher Layton (1966:18), Magdoff (1969:62) suggests that "in the three biggest European markets (West Germany, Britain, and France) 40 percent of United States direct investment is accounted for by three firms—Esso, General Motors, and Ford. In all western Europe, 20 United States firms account for two thirds of United States investment."

BANKING AND FINANCE

In conjunction with the enormously extended military presence and political influence of the United States and her domination of multinational corporate giants, an international financial system has emerged. If this system also is dominated by the United States and the dollar has evolved as the key international currency and reserve, no one should be surprised.

In his chapter entitled "The Banks and Their New Role," Lenin (1939) underscored the fact that the centralization of finance facilitated and went hand in hand with the concentration of industrial capital. In every advanced capitalist economy, a few giant banks extended a large and complex network of numerous branches at home and abroad.

In these respects, things have not changed much. Although the United States continues to penetrate and dominate foreign markets by means of foreign banks and subsidiary corporations, *branch banks* are especially profitable. Branch banks profit greatly "from United States international activities; [from] the money spent by United States armed forces abroad, the bank deposits arising from foreign aid, and the banking business that accompanies private investment abroad" (Magdoff, 1969:72). The branch bank is the primary means of effectively competing with the host country's institutions, thereby increasing the strength, wealth, and influence of a few giant U.S. banking firms that, together, control the expansion into foreign fields. The concentration of overseas investment in manufacturing and extractive industries in a few hands corresponds with the concentration of banking capital. Thus, by the end of 1967, the United States had 298 overseas branches located in 55 countries, 259 of which were "owned by three banks: First National City Bank, Chase Manhattan Bank, and Bank of America" (Magdoff, 1969:73).

It is especially interesting that these banks play an increasingly important role not only in the underdeveloped areas, but also in the industrialized countries of Europe as well. In this regard, Jeremy Main (1967:143) observed, in *Fortune* magazine that "it has become a cliché in banking circles to say that 'the only really European banks nowadays are American.'" Professor Charles B. Kindleberger (Magdoff, 1969:76) called attention to the remarkable fact that "of the commercial banks it is the United States institutions —Morgan Guaranty Trust Co., Chase Manhattan, First National City, in particular—which are represented in the several countries of the Common Market rather than European institutions."

Increasing U.S. domination of international finance has as a matter of course established the dollar as the world currency. Dissolution of the British empire in the aftermath of the Second World War and the decline of British leadership of the capitalist world simultaneously with assumption of that leadership by the United States may be traced in displacement of the pound by the dollar. This displacement has been so complete that the dollar has effectively joined and even replaced gold as the international monetary reserve. Equation of the dollar with gold means that all capitalist nations are dependent on the United States in varying degrees.

Clearly, the economic and military power of the United States has enabled the dollar to become what it has. In turn, the dollar, having become the world currency, has vastly enhanced United States economic and military strength. This is so because the United States overseas military presence, military aid, and economic assistance—the entire structure, in short, through which she maintains the capitalist world —rests on the other capitalist powers' acceptance of the international monetary system based on the dollar. Knowing that their fate is bound up with the fate of the United States and that the United States has the ability to act unilaterally to undermine the international system, all other capitalist powers behave as if the dollar were as good as gold.

There can be no doubt that this status of the dollar has given the United States untold advantages, enabling her, for example, to operate on a persistent balance-of-payments deficit with relative impunity. Being the world banker means that the United States can enrich itself considerably more than would be possible if the United States' trading partners refused its dollar IOUs and demanded gold instead. The hegemony of the dollar, then, is a manifestation of the United States leadership of the capitalist-industrial world. But the power of the United States has had its most telling consequences not so much among the industrialized nations as among the underdeveloped nations.

CONTINUED EXPLOITATION OF UNDERDEVELOPED COUNTRIES

The new imperialism of the United States does not require that she dominate the underdeveloped countries openly and directly in order to control and exploit them. Military assistance, private investment, and foreign-aid programs accomplish this end quite as well. The primary aims and consequences of economic and military assistance are to guarantee United States business interests complete access to natural resources as well as to trade and investment opportunities. Programs of economic and military assistance are also designed to yield direct profits for U.S. businessmen. Insofar as a limited economic development is allowed or fostered, it must further United States capital interests. Certainly, it must not depart significantly from accepted capitalist methods. Finally, United States assistance serves to perpetuate dependency of the country in question on United States capital and occasionally on the capital of other advanced industrial economies.

If, for example, we focus attention on Latin America, there can be no doubt that United States military assistance to the various regimes and juntas has nothing to do with the defense either of those countries or of the United States. Where, as is certainly true of Latin America, there is no threat of war among the countries themselves and no threat of war from any power external to the continent, the vast military arsenals that have been provided for these regimes can have only one purpose. That purpose is clear: to maintain the regimes of the rich and privileged few who, in turn, create a hospitable environment for U.S. business interests. This is facilitated by the United States government's support of these business interests and its alliance with the regimes of the Latin American landed and commercial oligarchies.

Because such an alliance inescapably implies that the given country will remain economically backward—or, at best,—that it will develop in a lopsided fashion suited only to the interests of foreign capital—it also necessarily means a perpetuation of the prevailing condition of the masses: poverty, squalor, and great suffering. Where this is the case, resistance, opposition, and violence are to be expected. Indeed, we all know that in Latin America (as elsewhere in the underdeveloped world) organized movements dedicated to far-reaching social changes do exist. Bridling or crushing these movements is the purpose for which the U.S. government so abundantly supplies the Latin American military with the most modern and lethal military hardware and trains its officer cadres.

In this regard, Magdoff (1969) speaks of a "symbiosis of U.S. and Latin American generals" and cites the Congressional testimony of General Robert W. Porter, Jr., U.S. Army Commander in Chief, U.S. Southern Command ("Southern" referring to all territory south of the United States). Noting the connection between the absence of economic development, general poverty, urban squalor, other serious social issues, and the Communists' attempt to exploit the issues, Porter (Magdoff, 1969:122) goes on to say:

> When added to the already-serious situation, this increasing urban threat will create a serious internal security problem for the governments of Latin America.
>
> The military has frequently proven to be the most cohesive force available to assure public order and support of resolute governments attempting to maintain internal security. Latin American armed forces, acting in conjunction with the police and other security forces, have helped to control disorders and riots, contained or eliminated terrorists and guerrillas, and discouraged those elements which are tempted to resort to violence to overthrow the government.

There it is frankly and candidly! United States military assistance to Latin American countries is not intended to counter any external military threat of Communism but to contain or destroy internal revolutionary movements and to keep those countries within the U.S. empire.

Economic assistance is similarly used not only to hold a country within the United States orbit, but to exact compliance with the wishes of private U.S. investors. Joan M. Nelson (1968:107–08) tells us, for instance, that when a new Peruvian government attempted to withdraw tax concessions from the International Petroleum Corporation, a subsidiary of Standard Oil of New Jersey, the United States withheld its aid until the government reversed its decision.

From the same source, we learn that the United States employs this lever not merely in Latin America but wherever it can as, for example, in Ceylon, when it nationalized gasoline stations owned by Esso Standard Eastern and Caltex Ceylon. And from the March 1, 1966 issue of *Forbes Magazine* (Magdoff, 1969:128) we learn:

> For a long time India insisted that it handle all the distribution of fertilizer produced in that country by U.S. companies and that it also set the price. Standard of Indiana understandably refused to accept these conditions. AID put food shipments to India on a month-to-month basis until the Indian government let Standard of Indiana market its fertilizer at its own prices.

Foreign aid, then, whether military or economic, is an instrument of control, a control that benefits certain U.S. business interests most directly. Alerting us to the fact that big businesses rely today on what amounts to a government subsidy, Magdoff (1969:129) cites the following statement by the administrative vice-president of the United States Steel Corporation:

> It is largely due to the operation of our foreign aid program that the steel industry has managed to escape the full effects of the forces at work in the world's market place. We estimate that AID procurement in the United States of steel mill products currently accounts for some 30 percent of the value of our steel exports, and for an even higher percent of the tonnage shipped—perhaps as much as 40 percent.

Not only do AID and other assistance programs enable United States corporations to sell commodities for which no markets otherwise would exist, but the programs also enable them to do so at prices well above world levels. In addition, by making military forces throughout dependent on standardized United States equipment, military assistance itself is a continuing source of profits for manufacturers of military hardware.

There is much more to say about foreign aid and the numerous ways in which it tends to perpetuate economic backwardness and dependency rather than to benefit the recipient. The interested reader should consult Magdoff's (1969) chapter entitled "Aid and Trade." Here, however, we will consider only one more important point.

Perhaps the most striking irony associated with United States' assistance to the underdeveloped areas is that upon careful examination, it turns out to be no assistance at all or, more precisely, it is United States assistance to itself. At least as far as Latin America is concerned, this appears definitely to be the case. According to Magdoff's (1969: 152–53) calculations,

> during the years 1962 to 1966, the average annual service payments on the external public debt of all Latin America was $1,596 million. During the same years, the average annual assistance from the United States to Latin American countries, in the forms of loans and grants, amounted to $1,213 [million]. Thus, economic assistance from the United States did not even cover the debt service requirements of Latin America as a whole!

ECONOMIC TAPROOT OF UNITED STATES IMPERIALISM

We have seen that securing foreign sources of raw material is absolutely essential to the United States economy. We have also seen that U.S. leadership in international finance brings with it substantial gains for U.S. business interests. Finally, we have noted the benefits these interests derive from military and economic foreign assistance programs. What remains for us to consider in this lamentably brief discussion is the putative connection between the market and investment needs of contemporary corporate capitalism and the new form of imperialism.

There are those who readily acknowledge the unprecedented expansion of United States military and political influence and power since the end of the Second World War. They even acknowledged that the United States dominates the underdeveloped areas of the world in various direct and indirect ways. Nevertheless, they insist that this is a matter of political policy dictated by security and other national interests. What they deny is that vested economic interests play a determining role in this policy. Since export and foreign investment constitute relatively minor elements in the total U.S. economy, these same people argue, these elements cannot be a major determinant of U.S. foreign policy. And if the present foreign policy of the United States is *not* based on any economic necessities, then it is not to the best interests of the nation and may more easily be changed.

The reader will recognize this general argument as similar to Hobson's. Hobson mobilized considerable evidence to support his view that Britain's trade with her empire was small, precarious and unprogressive. In the same vein, Hobson (1971:38–39) deduced:

> As for the territories acquired under the new Imperialism, except in one instance, no serious attempt to regard them as satisfactory business assets is possible. . . .

> At whatever figure we estimate the profits in this trade [with Great Britain's new possessions in Africa, Asia, and the Pacific], it forms an utterly insignificant part of our national income, while the expenses connected directly and indirectly with the acquisition, administration and defense of these possessions must swallow an immeasurably larger sum.

These observations convinced Hobson that imperialism was definitely opposed to the best economic interests of the bulk of the nation; for this reason, he deemed the abolition of imperialism, by means of reform, both desirable and possible. However, he recognized that this would be far from a simple matter.

From the fact that a relative minority gained most directly from imperialism it did not follow that imperialism would be easy to abolish. Hobson (1971:48) emphasized that "a State in which certain well-organized business interests are able to outweigh the weak, diffused interest of the community is bound to pursue a policy which accords with the pressure of the former interests." The power of these business interests ought not to be dismissed by arguing that they are a small minority; they are organized to gain from imperialism and militarism, to work their will in the arena of politics, and to resist forces of change. Today, some seventy years after Hobson presented his thesis, we know that the extent to which British imperial domination has been brought to an end has not been achieved by popular and democratic reforms of British society.

A similar logic may be applied to U.S. imperialism. Even if foreign trade and investment constitute a minor element of the total economy and, accordingly, only a relative minority benefits, this would not *necessarily* mean that the imperialist policy is less tenacious. And if imperialism is strong under these circumstances, how much greater must its power and tenacity be if the economic stake in imperialism is substantially greater than has been estimated? This is precisely the point that Magdoff wishes to demonstrate: United States foreign investment and trade are not as minor as some have believed them to be.

Magdoff stresses that it is most important to understand that the United States interest in foreign business is not adequately reflected in the volume of commodity exports. The accumulation of capital abroad has proceeded at a much more rapid rate than exports have. One must bear in mind that

> the annual flow of capital invested abroad is . . . additive: increments to capital enlarge the productive base. Even more important, United States firms abroad are able to mobilize foreign capital for their operations. The net result of the flow of capital abroad and the foreign capital mobilized by American firms is that while production abroad

arising out of United States investment was 4½ times larger than exports in 1950, by 1964 this had risen to 5½ times exports (Magdoff, 1969: 177).

Magdoff shows that United States foreign economic activity grew in importance appreciably from 1950 to 1964, with foreign sales (exports plus sales of foreign-based firms) rising more rapidly than sales of domestic firms. In a like manner, U.S. expenditures for the plant and equipment of its subsidiaries abroad increased from 8.1 percent (of the investment of domestic manufacturing firms) in 1957 to 17.3 percent in 1965.

Expanding profits from foreign operations also are important to consider. These rose from 10 percent of domestic nonfinancial corporate profits after taxes in 1950 to 22 percent in 1964. In general, there can be no doubt of the rapid growth of foreign business: "For example, in manufacturing industries during the past ten years [1955–64] domestic sales increased by 50 percent, while foreign sales by United States-owned factories increased over 110 percent" (Magdoff, 1969:183).

Also, there can be no doubt that the giant corporations are primarily involved in foreign business: "Just a cursory examination of the 50 largest industrial concerns shows the following types of firms heavily involved in international economic operations and the supply of military goods: 12 in oil, 5 in aviation, 3 in chemicals, 3 in steel, 3 in autos, 8 in electrical equipment and electronics, and 3 in rubber. These 37 companies account for over 90 percent of the assets of the top 50 industrial firms" (Magdoff, 1969:191). Can one doubt, then, that these giants have a profound influence on foreign policy—not to mention the multitude of smaller businesses involved in military production as subcontractors?

10

A Brief Comment on
the War in Indo-China
and the Relevance
of the Theory of Imperialism

There are today intelligent critics and dedicated opponents of the expanding war economy of the United States who deny that militarization and war have anything to do with imperialism. Seymour Melman (1970:155–56), for example, insists that "the classic theories of economic imperialism fail to explain the behavior of the United States in Vietnam. There is no evidence of recent or planned trade or investment in Vietnam by major U.S. firms of the sort and the scale that might prompt an effort to bring substantial pressure on United States government policy."

For Melman, the view that the major U.S. industrial

and financial firms have had a large stake in the war and have therefore pressed for its perpetuation is totally untenable. Why? Because

> the available evidence points to the direction of major formal control coming primarily from the Department of Defense to these firms, not in a reverse direction. . . .
> In sum the family of theories that would explain the Vietnam War as the result of one or another group of private firms using the government as an instrument for their advantage fails for lack of evidence.
>   The existence and normal operation of a state-management over military industry, at the peak position of the federal government, offers a more fruitful explanation of Pentagon and federal government behavior (Melman, 1970:156–57).

The essentials of Melman's more general thesis are that the concentration of power in the United States has gone considerably beyond the point C. Wright Mills (1959) described in his *Power Elite*. Mills argued convincingly that a system of power that consisted of the economic, political and military elites had emerged in the United States. These three elites stood in a coordinate relation to one another. Whether one or the other led or followed depended on a variety of complex international and domestic conditions. In the historical context of the time (the mid-1950s), the military appeared to be gaining strength. In Mills' (1959: 277) words:

> Today all three are involved in virtually all widely ramifying decisions. Which of the three types seems to lead depends upon "the tasks of the period" as they, the elite, define them. Just now, these tasks center upon "defense" and international affairs. Accordingly, as we have seen, the military are ascendant in two senses: as personnel and as justifying ideology. That is why, just now, we can most easily specify the unity and the shape

of the power elite in terms of the military ascendancy.

This analysis of a developing military capitalism, Melman believes, was accurate for the 1950s. This was a period
of transition, which came to a close with President Eisenhower's now famous farewell address in which he warned
the nation that "In the councils of government we must
guard against the acquisition of unwarranted influence,
whether sought or unsought, by the military-industrial
complex. The potential for the disastrous rise of misplaced
power exists and will persist."

Eisenhower's warning went unheeded. Steadily expanding its wealth and power, the military-industrial complex
today has assumed the proportions of a gigantic parastate
—a state within a state that has continually extended its
control over means of production, the universities, and research. This Behemoth has fabricated and perpetuated the
myths and ideology of "defense" and has led the nation
into the Vietnam disaster. In a sense, then, Melman sees
himself extending Mills' analysis and adapting it to the
1960s.

Let me make myself unmistakably clear: I believe that
much of Melman's analysis is correct. He documents how a
military capitalism is gathering momentum in this country,
how the economy is becoming a war economy, quite amply.

Let me also emphasize that in criticizing Melman, I am
not defending what Mills (1959) correctly labeled as a
"simple Marxian view [which] makes the big economic
man the *real* holder of power." I wholeheartedly agree with
Mills that "we must always be historically specific and open
to complexities." Indeed, my criticism of Melman's work is
that he overlooks certain historically specific complexities
that led to the war in Vietnam and its prolongation and that
he fails to grasp fully the implications of Mills' thesis.

No doubt it is true, as Melman shows, that the parastate
has sustained and expanded itself by selling fear—notably,
fear of Communism "as a lever for prying more and more
support from the public and Congress for ever-larger mili-

tary budgets. Here is the list of defense inadequacies that the operators of the most powerful military machine in the world claim to have existed since 1960: "missile gap, bomber gap, anti-ballistic missile gap, fighter plane gap, megatonnage gap, submarine gap, survival gap, strategy gap, security gap" (Melman, 1970:225–26). It is also quite possible, as Melman maintains, that the channels of formal control proceed from the Pentagon to the corporations, not vice versa. Finally, it appears to be true that a militarily dominated parastate has become the major determinant of the destruction and depletion of human and material resources and the general deterioration of the quality of life. The parastate creates international crises and war and these, in turn, greatly enhance its power. Thus, Melman underscores an even greater ascendancy of the military since Mills wrote— so much so that the Pentagon has become an independent variable.

Clearly, Melman recognizes not only the militarization of the economy but also the fact that the primary and most direct beneficiaries of this trend have been the big corporations. Appendix E of his book (1970:259–60) provides an index of 100 companies that, together with their subsidiaries, "received the largest dollar volume of military prime contract awards in fiscal year 1968." Of course, this list includes the most well-known U.S. corporate giants. Melman is therefore confirming, not denying, that the giant corporations have a substantial stake in military capitalism.

Melman also acknowledges that the corporations have substantial private long-term investments abroad. However, Melman dismisses the interest in foreign private investment and markets as a factor in both the militarization of the economy and the war on three counts: first, the bulk of these investments are in Canada and Western Europe; second, their total value as of 1966 was 54.2 billions of dollars—less than the 100 billion dollars already spent on the Vietnam war, and, finally, because no one has demonstrated potential or actual investments in Vietnam.

In addition, Melman (1970:157–58) dismisses the factor of foreign private investment but draws attention to the parastate's military-political interventionist strategy, including:

1. Support of friendly governments.
2. Buying allies (and elections).
3. Supporting military coups at a distance.
4. Supporting military coups by intervention.
5. Physical occupation of a territory.
6. Subduing an opponent by military force.

Thus, according to Melman, a military-political imperialism is generated into being, sustained, and expanded by the parastate's successful manufacture and sale of myths and fear. Economic interests play no role here. The corporations do, in fact, have a stake in the war economy, but this stake is assured by the perpetually expanding military budget and fat cost-plus contracts. Nevertheless, the corporations have neither a short-range nor a long-range interest in foreign domination, intervention and war. This is so because the state management guarantees an enlarged military budget even after the Vietnam war in order to replenish depleted inventories, to develop new military systems, and so forth.

This is the way in which Melman tries to separate economic from military and political interests and denies that the corporations have any real interest in United States political-military imperialism. This curious view merits a closer look.

I assume that when the United States has either intervened or attempted to intervene in the affairs of another country (politically or militarily, directly or indirectly) and it can be shown that U.S. businesses have substantial investments in that country, Melman would not deny that economic interest undoubtedly constituted some component of the decision to intervene. A few of the most well-known examples that come to mind are U.S. intervention in Guatemala, Cuba, and the Dominican Republic.

I also assume that Melman would not question the role of economic interests in, for example, domination of Indo-

China by France or her prolonged but futile war to maintain its hold, culminating in her defeat at Dienbienphu. In this case, consideration of economic interests is beyond doubt. In contrast, what is striking about the United States' presence in Vietnam is the absence of actual investments. Melman rejects all attempts to explain the war in terms of economic imperialism precisely because of this factor.

The trouble with this reasoning is that it is mechanistic and therefore fails to get at the heart of the issue. It is mechanistic because (1) it treats the Vietnam war as an event unto itself, separate and disconnected from the whole of U.S. foreign policy; (2) it seeks to separate economic from political and military interests, thus failing to grasp the essential unity of these interests; and (3) it ignores the historical circumstances in which the United States began to involve itself in Vietnam.

Melman looks at Vietnam and, discerning that the U.S. has no substantial concrete investments there, he concludes that the war is not a result of "economic" imperialism. But of course! Certainly, U.S. intervention in Vietnam was not purely for economic reasons, nor were her expansion and intervention in other places merely for economic, for political, or for military purposes.

If Melman had recognized that the long-range strategy of United States foreign policy is to prevent the further contraction of the capitalist world and that the goal is in the most direct interest of *all* the dominant components of the power elite, he would not have asserted that the potential control of Vietnam has no economic significance.

The fall of Dienbienphu and the ousting of the French created a political vacuum. Would it be filled by the non-capitalist forces represented by Ho chi minh or by the allies and clients of the United States government? If the former had occurred, the United States could never have done business in that country on its own terms. If, on the other hand, South Vietnam were drawn securely into the U.S. orbit, that country could be shaped in the capitalistic image. Melman may have difficulty in accepting this conception of things, but some leading U.S. businessmen have not. In 1965, the vice-president in charge of Far Eastern operations of Chase Manhattan Bank expressed this view:

> In the past, foreign investors have been some-what wary of the over-all political prospect for the [Southeast Asia] region. I must say, though, that the U.S. actions in Vietnam this year—which have demonstrated that the U.S. will continue to give effective protection to the free nations of the region—have considerably reassured both Asian and Western investors. In fact, I see some reason for hope that the same sort of economic growth may take place in the free economies of Asia that took place in Europe after the Truman Doctrine and after NATO provided a protective shield. The same thing also took place in Japan after the U.S. intervention in Korea removed investor doubts (quoted in Magdoff, 1969:176).

This statement unequivocally affirms the inseparability of the economic, political, and military components of present-day U.S. foreign policy. Southeast Asia is no exception.

Concluding Remarks

For many of the questions raised in this essay there are no simple answers, nor can the validity of alternative answers be demonstrated in any simple scientific sense. The best one can do is to make as cogent a case as possible. This in fact has been our aim.

We have raised significant questions and suggested how one might approach them from a so-called neo-Marxian perspective. The label is unimportant. What is important is to understand this perspective and to take it seriously in thinking through the major issues facing us all.

I use the term "perspective" although "approach" may be equally appropriate. As the reader undoubtedly has noticed, my essay presents no simple formula; rather, it suggests a way of approaching complex problems and issues.

The spirit of this approach is analytical, open, and critical—*analytical* in that it encourages thinking and opposes easy answers, *open* in that it abhors closed or dogmatic systems, and *critical* in that it helps one see through the more prevalent viewpoints, particularly how one-sided, misleading, and inadequate they are. This is the spirit in which I intended this essay and it is in the same spirit, I hope, that the reader has received it. If after pondering the argument developed in these pages the reader is moved to pursue further the issues raised, I will have accomplished my principal purpose.

References

Baran, Paul, and Paul Sweezy
    1966   Monopoly Capital. New York: Monthly Review
        Press.
Berle, Adolph A.
    1954   The Twentieth Century Capitalist Revolution. New
        York: Harcourt, Brace & Co.
Berle, Adolph A., and Gardiner C. Means
    1967   The Modern Corporation and Private Property.
        New York: Harcourt, Brace & Co.
Bright, Arthur A.
    1949   The Electric Lamp Industry. New York: Macmil-
        lan.
Christman, Henry M., ed.
    1966   The American Journalism of Marx and Engels.
        New York: New American Library.
Clark, Colin
    1940   The Conditions of Economic Progress. London:
        Macmillan & Co.

Earley, James S.
1957 "Marginal power of 'excellently managed' companies." American Economic Review (March): 333–35.
Fortune
1961 "The incredible electrical conspiracy." (May).
Hamberg, Daniel
1956 Economic Growth and Instability. New York: Norton.
Hilferding, Rudolf
1968 Das Finanzkapital. Frankfort: Europäische Verlagsanstalt.
Hobson, J. A.
1971 Imperialism. Ann Arbor: University of Michigan Press.
Layton, Christopher
1966 Trans-Atlantic Investment. Boulogne-sur Seine, France.
Lenin, Vladimir I.
1939 Imperialism: The Highest Stage of Capitalism. New York: International Publishers.
Machlup, Fritz
1952 The Political Economy of Monopoly. Baltimore: Johns Hopkins Press.
Magdoff, Harry
1969 The Age of Imperialism. New York: Monthly Review Press.
Main, Jeremy
1967 "The first real international bankers." Fortune (December).
Mandel, Ernest
1968 Marxist Economic Theory. Vol. I. Brian Pearce, translator. New York and London: Monthly Review Press.
Marx, Karl
1853 "The future results of British rule in India." New York Daily Tribune (July 22). Reprinted in Henry R. Christman, ed. The American Journal-

ism of Marx and Engels. New York: New American Library, 1966.

Marx, Karl
1962   Capital. Vol. I, Process of Capitalist Production as a Whole. Moscow: Foreign Languages Publishing House.

Marx, Karl, and Friedrich Engels
1953a   Selected Correspondence. Moscow: Foreign Languages Publishing House.

Marx, Karl, and Friedrich Engels
1953b   On Britain. Moscow: Foreign Languages Publishing House.

Melman, Seymour
1970   Pentagon Capitalism. New York: McGraw-Hill.

Mills, C. Wright
1956   The Power Elite. New York: Oxford University Press.

Nelson, Joan M.
1968   Aid, Influence, and Foreign Policy. New York: Macmillan.

Robinson, Edward A.
1952   Monopoly. Cambridge, Mass.: Cambridge University Press.

Scitovsky, Tibor
1951   Welfare and Competition: The Economics of a Fully Employed Economy. Chicago: Irwin.

Sternberg, Fritz
1946   The Coming Crisis. New York: John Day.

Stocking, George W., and Myron W. Watkins
1950   Monopoly and Free Enterprise. New York: Twentieth Century Fund.

Sweezy, Paul
1942   The Theory of Capitalist Development. New York: Monthly Review Press.

U.S. Bureau of the Census, Department of Commerce
1960   Historical Statistics of the United States: Colonial Times to 1957. Washington, D.C.: U.S. Government Printing Office.

U.S. Bureau of the Census, Department of Commerce
  1963   "Raw materials in the U.S. economy, 1900–1961."
         United States Bureau of the Census Working Pa-
         per no. 6. Washington, D.C.: U.S. Government
         Printing Office.
Woytinskii, Wladimir
  1936   "The social consequences of the economic depres-
         sion." Studies and Reports, Series C (Employ-
         ment and Unemployment) no. 21. Geneva: Inter-
         national Labor Office.

Index